The Nonprofit Operations Playbook

Understanding Nonprofit Operations for Mission-
Driven Organizations

Matthew B. Scraper

Disclaimers and Copyright Information

ISBN 978-1-304-11337-5
Imprint: Lulu.com

Copyright Information

Publisher Information

Published by Lulu Press, Inc.
For more information, visit **www.lulu.com**.

Disclaimer

The information provided in this book is based on the author's personal experiences, research, and professional expertise. While every effort has been made to ensure accuracy and relevance, this book is not intended as legal, financial, or professional advice. Readers are encouraged to seek appropriate counsel for their specific circumstances.

The opinions expressed in this book are solely those of the author and do not necessarily reflect the views of any organizations, institutions, or individuals mentioned within.

Acknowledgments
The author has made every effort to acknowledge and credit all sources and references used in this book. Any omissions or errors are unintentional and will be corrected in future editions, if notified.

Trademarks
All trademarks, service marks, product names, or named features mentioned in this book are the property of their respective owners. Use of these names does not imply any affiliation or endorsement.

Contact Information
For inquiries, permissions, or additional resources, visit **www.mbsoperations.com**.

First Edition
Printed in the United States of America

Table of Contents

Contents

Part 1: Foundation and Framework

Chapter 1: The Unique Role of a COO in the Nonprofit Sector

The nonprofit Chief Operating Officer (COO) is often a silent force behind an organization's mission, ensuring that every operational detail aligns with the overarching purpose. It's a role that demands a delicate balance between vision and logistics, strategy and execution. Unlike the COO in a for-profit corporation, whose primary focus may be maximizing shareholder value, the nonprofit COO must navigate the complexities of aligning resources, people, and processes to achieve impact—all while staying true to the organization's values.

When I first stepped into a COO role, I quickly realized that the job is as much about heart as it is about head. My journey has spanned various organizations, from leading operations at Faith in Public Life to my work as a fractional COO supporting nonprofits and churches across the country. Along the way, I've developed policies to address real-world challenges, implemented systems that save time and money, and navigated crises that tested the limits of organizational resilience. Each experience has deepened my understanding of what it means to manage a mission-driven organization.

This book is not only a practical guide but also a gateway into a broader series of resources for nonprofit leaders. It serves as an entry point into a comprehensive suite of works that build on each other to support nonprofit success. If you've read **Effective Nonprofit Board Governance** (for a deeper understanding of board engagement) or **Policies and Procedures for Nonprofit Success** (for a closer look at governance and policy creation), you'll find this book provides the essential operational backdrop. Those seeking to start a nonprofit can find a strong foundation in **How to Start a Nonprofit (and Actually Succeed!) A Step-by-Step Guide for Visionaries and Changemakers,** which walks early-stage founders through the formative steps of nonprofit creation.

Each of these works is designed to stand alone, but together they form a cohesive library for nonprofit excellence. This book focuses on the COO's role—the central architect of operational excellence—while offering practical insights, personal reflections, and actionable steps to strengthen your leadership capacity.

The Evolution of the COO Role in Nonprofit Organizations

Historically, nonprofits often relied on passionate leaders to manage every aspect of their operations, assuming the mission itself would drive success. Over time, however, it became clear that passion alone wasn't enough. Complex financial regulations, increasing scrutiny from funders, and the rapid pace of technological change necessitated a new kind of leader: one who could build and maintain the structures needed to sustain the mission.

The COO role has since evolved into one of the most critical positions in nonprofit leadership. Today's COOs must wear many hats—strategist, problem-solver, innovator, and mentor—while working in close partnership with the CEO, board, and staff. For example, at Faith in Public Life, I helped institute operational policies like progressive discipline procedures and emergency protocols that not only stabilized the organization but also ensured equity and transparency. These initiatives demonstrated how operational rigor can amplify, rather than detract from, a nonprofit's values.

Balancing Mission-Driven Leadership with Operational Excellence

Being a COO in the nonprofit sector means walking a tightrope between two worlds. On one side is the mission, the beating heart of the organization, which inspires staff, funders, and stakeholders to invest their time and resources. On the other side is operational excellence, the framework that ensures that the mission is more than just a dream. Without strong systems and processes, even the most compelling mission will falter.

This balance was especially evident when I led the accreditation process for the Standards for Excellence at the Oklahoma Center for Nonprofits. It required not only meeting rigorous operational benchmarks but also ensuring that those benchmarks reflected our organization's core values. The process underscored a critical truth: operational discipline doesn't detract from a nonprofit's mission—it strengthens it.

At Faith in Public Life, this balance also showed up in the transition from using external accountants to hiring an internal Director of Finance. By taking on the operational challenge of managing our own financial systems, we not only saved money but also gained deeper insights into how our resources could better serve our mission. These examples highlight how a COO's work behind the scenes can create a foundation for transformative impact.

An Overview of the Book's Themes

This book is a guide for nonprofit COOs and aspiring operational leaders who want to navigate the complexities of their role with confidence and purpose. It focuses on four key areas:

1. **Strategic Planning**: Understanding how to bridge the gap between an organization's mission and its daily operations, with insights on creating sustainable, actionable plans.

2. **People Management**: Building a resilient and motivated team through effective feedback, professional development, and equitable HR practices.

3. **Financial Stewardship**: Developing and managing budgets, overseeing compliance, and using tools like dashboards to inform decision-making.

4. **Operational Resilience**: Preparing for and responding to crises, from emergency protocols to facility management.

Each chapter draws from my personal experiences, offering practical tools, case studies, and insights to help you lead with both heart and strategy. Whether you're tackling the nuances of strategic planning or the intricacies of cybersecurity, this book will equip you to navigate the challenges of nonprofit operations while staying grounded in your organization's mission.

Nonprofit work is never easy, but it's profoundly rewarding. As you dive into the chapters ahead, I encourage you to embrace both the challenges and the opportunities of your role. Together, we'll explore how operational excellence can be a powerful catalyst for mission-driven impact.

Chapter 2: The Role of a COO and Operational Leadership in Nonprofits

Defining the COO's Role

The Chief Operating Officer (COO) plays a pivotal role in the daily operations and strategic execution of a nonprofit organization. Unlike the Executive Director (ED) or Chief Executive Officer (CEO), whose focus leans more on external relations and strategic vision, the COO's role is deeply rooted in operational efficiency, systems management, and internal coordination.

Core Responsibilities of the COO

1. **Operational Oversight:** The COO is responsible for the internal operations of the organization, including human resources, technology, facilities, finance, and compliance. This person ensures that daily operations are aligned with the nonprofit's strategic goals and that all departments are functioning efficiently.

2. **Strategic Execution:** While the CEO sets the vision, the COO ensures it becomes reality. This role involves translating high-level strategy into actionable operational plans, setting departmental goals, and tracking progress.

3. **Change Management:** Nonprofits frequently undergo changes related to funding, technology, and staffing. The COO leads change management

efforts, ensuring smooth transitions and minimizing disruptions.

4. **Internal Collaboration:** The COO serves as a bridge between different departments, fostering cross-functional collaboration. This role requires high emotional intelligence and the ability to mediate conflicts and align teams toward shared goals.

5. **Performance Management:** From overseeing employee development to ensuring staff adhere to organizational policies, the COO plays a significant role in employee performance and accountability.

6. **Financial Stewardship:** The COO often works closely with the Chief Financial Officer (CFO) to oversee budgeting, financial planning, and cost management. While the CFO manages financial reports, the COO ensures that resources are used efficiently.

Why the COO Role is Critical

The COO's influence extends beyond operational efficiency—they drive organizational sustainability. By ensuring that systems, people, and processes are aligned, the COO creates a stable foundation for growth. In many nonprofits, especially those experiencing rapid growth or facing operational complexity, the COO's role becomes indispensable.

Balancing Strategy and Tactics

A hallmark of an effective COO is their ability to balance strategy with tactics. While strategy provides the "what" and "why" of an organization's objectives, tactics focus on "how" those objectives are achieved.

Strategic Responsibilities

1. **Mission Alignment:** The COO ensures all operational activities are mission-driven. For example, if a nonprofit's mission is to provide housing for underserved communities, the COO will ensure that procurement, staffing, and facilities management support that mission.

2. **Data-Driven Decisions:** The COO relies on dashboards, Key Performance Indicators (KPIs), and financial metrics to make informed decisions. This approach allows them to identify trends and adjust operational tactics accordingly.

3. **Capacity Building:** As nonprofits grow, so does the need for scalable infrastructure. The COO ensures that systems, software, and staffing capacity are prepared for growth.

4. **Risk Management:** The COO identifies and mitigates potential risks, from cybersecurity threats to compliance violations. Their proactive stance protects the organization's reputation and financial health.

Tactical Responsibilities

1. **Process Improvement:** The COO creates and refines standard operating procedures (SOPs) for

repetitive tasks such as donor acknowledgments, grant reporting, and procurement.

2. **Project Management:** Whether launching a new donor CRM or implementing a new payroll system, the COO ensures that projects stay on time and within budget.

3. **Workforce Coordination:** From scheduling to staff deployment, the COO ensures that human resources are deployed in the most efficient way possible. This role often requires scheduling cross-departmental projects and ensuring deadlines are met.

4. **Technology Integration:** Technology is central to operational efficiency. The COO manages the implementation of new technology platforms and ensures staff are properly trained.

By balancing strategy and tactics, the COO ensures that day-to-day operations align with broader organizational goals. Their ability to "zoom in and out" of operational issues allows them to remain agile in response to changes in the nonprofit landscape.

Key Operational Leadership Skills and Attributes

To excel as a COO in a nonprofit, certain skills and personal attributes are essential. Nonprofit operations are complex, often requiring leaders to juggle limited resources while maximizing impact.

Essential Skills

1. **Systems Thinking:** Nonprofits operate as interconnected systems—finance, human resources, fundraising, and programming are all interdependent. A successful COO sees these connections and optimizes the whole system rather than focusing on isolated parts.

2. **Project Management:** From launching new initiatives to overhauling IT infrastructure, COOs must have strong project management skills, ensuring tasks are delivered on time, within scope, and within budget.

3. **Data Literacy:** COOs must interpret financial reports, operational dashboards, and HR analytics. Being able to use this data to inform decisions is critical to improving operational efficiency.

4. **Communication:** The COO must communicate with diverse stakeholders—from the Board of Directors to entry-level employees—and ensure messages are clear, concise, and aligned with organizational goals.

5. **Conflict Resolution:** Given their role in overseeing departments, COOs must resolve conflicts between teams or individuals. Mediation skills help maintain positive working relationships.

6. **Agility and Adaptability:** Nonprofits operate in an ever-changing environment. The COO must quickly

adapt to new regulations, shifting funding streams, or unexpected organizational crises.

Key Attributes

1. **Empathy and Emotional Intelligence (EQ):** Nonprofits are people-driven organizations, and staff are often motivated by the mission. A COO with high emotional intelligence will understand staff motivations, foster well-being, and encourage collaboration.

2. **Decisiveness:** Nonprofits face complex problems that require timely decision-making. A COO's ability to analyze situations quickly and act decisively can prevent operational bottlenecks.

3. **Accountability:** As the person responsible for operational execution, a COO must hold themselves and their teams accountable for meeting deadlines and achieving goals.

4. **Vision and Foresight:** While much of the COO's role is operational, they must also have a forward-looking perspective. They identify future opportunities and challenges, ensuring the organization is well-positioned for growth.

5. **Technical Acumen:** COOs often oversee IT, HR, and Finance—areas requiring a technical understanding of software systems, compliance regulations, and data security protocols.

6. **Resilience and Stress Tolerance:** Nonprofit work can be unpredictable, with unexpected crises,

funding delays, or leadership transitions. The COO must remain calm under pressure and guide the organization through uncertainty.

Conclusion

The role of a COO in a nonprofit is as dynamic as it is essential. COOs oversee internal operations, ensure strategic alignment, and create operational efficiencies that drive mission success. Balancing strategy with tactical execution requires a unique blend of skills, from data analysis and project management to emotional intelligence and adaptability. Nonprofit COOs are not just operational leaders—they are mission stewards, ensuring that every system, process, and policy contributes to the nonprofit's greater purpose. Through their leadership, nonprofits can scale impact, improve sustainability, and deliver lasting change in the communities they serve.

Chapter 3: Strategic vs. Tactical Planning - Bridging the Mission-Operations Gap

Defining Strategy vs. Tactics

One of the most essential concepts for nonprofit leaders to understand is the distinction between strategic planning and tactical planning. While they are interconnected, they serve distinct purposes within an organization. Strategic planning is the "why" and "what" — the high-level, long-term goals that guide the nonprofit toward its mission. Tactical planning, on the other hand, focuses on the "how" — the specific, actionable steps needed to achieve those strategic goals.

Strategic Planning

- **Purpose**: Defines the organization's mission, vision, and long-term goals.

- **Scope**: Broad, long-term focus (typically 3-5 years).

- **Questions Answered**: Why do we exist? What are our goals? What does success look like?

- **Responsibility**: Primarily the board and executive leadership.

Tactical Planning

- **Purpose**: Breaks down strategic goals into specific tasks and timelines.

- **Scope**: Narrow, short-term focus (usually 1 year or less).

- **Questions Answered**: How do we achieve our goals? What tasks must be completed? Who is responsible for each action?

- **Responsibility**: Operational staff, teams, and managers.

To illustrate the difference, imagine a nonprofit's strategic goal is to "increase food security in rural communities by 25% over five years." The tactical plan might outline the specific actions required, such as "launch five mobile food pantry sites within 12 months" and "develop partnerships with three local food distributors."

The Role of the Board vs. the COO

Understanding the roles of the board and the Chief Operating Officer (COO) in planning is essential for effective nonprofit governance. Role clarity prevents confusion, streamlines operations, and promotes mission alignment.

The Role of the Board

- **Focus**: Strategic oversight.

- **Responsibilities**:

  o Define the mission and vision.

  o Set the strategic direction and approve long-term goals.

  o Monitor progress toward strategic goals.

- o Support the executive team in achieving the organization's mission.

- **Key Distinction**: The board focuses on "what" and "why" but does not manage "how" tasks are executed.

The Role of the COO

- **Focus**: Tactical execution.

- **Responsibilities**:
  - o Translate strategic goals into operational plans.
  - o Lead staff to execute specific tactical objectives.
  - o Ensure alignment of day-to-day activities with the strategic plan.
  - o Manage deadlines, resources, and project tracking.

- **Key Distinction**: The COO is responsible for "how" the work gets done and "who" is responsible for each task.

When the roles of the board and COO are clearly defined, nonprofits can avoid the common pitfall of "role confusion" where boards delve too deeply into operations or where operational staff attempt to set high-level strategy.

Planning Role Matrix

Role/Responsibility	Board	Executive Leadership	Chief Operating Officer (COO)	Staff/Teams
Set Mission & Vision	Yes	Provides Input	Not Responsible	Not Responsible
Set Strategic Goals	Yes	Co-Develops	Not Responsible	Not Responsible
Approve Strategic Plan	Yes	Recommends	Not Responsible	Not Responsible
Create Tactical Plans	Not Responsible	Provides Oversight	Leads Development	Provides Input
Execute Tactical Plans	Not Responsible	Not Responsible	Manages Execution	Completes Tasks
Track Progress	Reviews	Monitors	Oversees Tracking	Reports Progress
Adjust Plans	Approves Adjustments	Recommends Adjustment	Executes Adjustments	Provides Input

Case Study from Faith in Public Life

The distinction between strategic and tactical planning is evident in real-life nonprofit operations. One example comes from Faith in Public Life's (FPL) decision to bring financial management in-house. The strategic goal, set by the board and executive team, was to "transition from an external accounting firm to internal financial management led by a Director of Finance." The COO's role was to create and execute a tactical plan for achieving that goal. This included:

- Drafting a job description for the Director of Finance.

- Managing the recruitment and hiring process.

- Setting up internal systems for financial reporting.

- Overseeing the onboarding of the new Director of Finance.

By keeping the board focused on strategy and allowing the COO to lead tactical execution, Faith in Public Life avoided role confusion, kept the project on schedule, and successfully completed the transition.

Key Takeaways for Nonprofit Leaders

1. **Strategic and Tactical Planning are Interdependent**: Strategy sets the "what" and "why," while tactics address "how" and "when."

2. **Role Clarity is Essential**: Boards set strategy, COOs lead execution, and staff complete operational tasks.

3. **Use a Role Matrix**: Define responsibilities for strategic and tactical planning to avoid role confusion.

4. **Case Studies Provide Insight**: The Faith in Public Life case shows how effective planning roles can drive successful outcomes.

By mastering the balance between strategic vision and tactical execution, nonprofit leaders ensure their organizations remain agile, effective, and mission-driven. This clear delineation of roles empowers leaders at every level to focus on their most impactful work.

Chapter 4: Mission-Driven Operations - Aligning Process with Purpose

Why Mission Alignment Matters in Operations

Imagine the mission of a nonprofit as the very heartbeat that sustains its life—a central force that gives purpose and direction to every program, campaign, and internal decision. For Chief Operating Officers (COOs) and other operational leaders, ensuring that daily operations remain true to this mission is both an art and a science. It's about making certain that the "why" behind the work is never lost in the "how" of execution. Prioritizing mission alignment allows organizations to not only achieve greater impact but also to strengthen stakeholder trust and cultivate a unified, purpose-driven internal culture.

Without mission alignment, nonprofits risk drifting from their purpose, especially when resource constraints or urgent challenges arise. Operational misalignment can lead to inefficiencies, wasted resources, and confusion among staff and stakeholders. For this reason, aligning operations with the mission must be intentional and systematic.

Key Operational Policies and Practices That Drive Alignment

1. **Operational Policies that Reflect Mission**

   o **Purpose:** Policies are the guardrails that keep operations mission-aligned. They ensure consistency, transparency, and equity in every organizational action.

- o **How to Do It:** Review all existing policies with a mission-first lens. Ask, "Does this policy reflect our core values and support our mission?" If not, revise it.

- o **Example:** At Faith in Public Life, I developed a progressive discipline procedure that balanced accountability with equity and compassion. While it provided clear steps for addressing performance issues, it also emphasized coaching and improvement over punitive measures. This approach embodied our commitment to justice and fairness.

2. **Mission-Driven Financial Stewardship**

- o **Purpose:** Every financial decision must be viewed as an opportunity to advance the mission. Mission-aligned financial stewardship prioritizes equity, accessibility, and transparency.

- o **How to Do It:** Create budgets that support mission-critical activities, avoid excess administrative overhead, and ensure resource allocation reflects organizational priorities.

- o **Example:** When Faith in Public Life transitioned from external accountants to an internal Director of Finance, the goal was to enhance control, transparency, and mission alignment. With an internal financial leader who understood our mission, we could ensure every dollar was spent in service to our larger purpose.

3. **Technology that Serves the Mission**

   o **Purpose:** Technology should support, not dictate, mission-driven work. The right tools amplify impact and efficiency.

   o **How to Do It:** Invest in mission-aligned technology tools that enable collaboration, improve impact measurement, and enhance program delivery.

   o **Example:** At FPL, the adoption of Salesforce was driven by a single question: "How will this help us fulfill our mission?" This approach guided every implementation decision, ensuring the system was customized for nonprofit needs. We also used Asana for cross-departmental collaboration, ensuring that workflows promoted teamwork and shared accountability.

4. **Staffing with Purpose**

   o **Purpose:** People are the most important asset of a mission-driven organization. Staff recruitment, development, and retention should align with the mission.

- How to Do It: Incorporate mission-driven principles into every step of the employee experience, from recruitment to performance reviews.

- Example: At Faith in Public Life, onboarding processes included cross-departmental introductions, helping staff understand how their role connected to the mission. New hires met with each department to see the "big picture," fostering a sense of shared purpose.

5. **Measuring Mission Impact**

- **Purpose:** It's not enough to assume mission alignment—you must measure it. Metrics must reflect progress toward mission-related goals, not just operational efficiency.

- **How to Do It:** Develop key performance indicators (KPIs) that measure mission-driven outcomes (not just outputs) and collect both qualitative and quantitative data.

- **Example:** At the Oklahoma Center for Nonprofits, we used dashboards to track attendance, satisfaction, and participant impact for training programs. In advocacy campaigns at Faith in Public Life, we went beyond media impressions to assess how campaigns aligned with the faith values of our stakeholders.

The Concept of "Operationalizing Values"

Operationalizing values is about turning lofty ideals into tangible, everyday actions. It's not enough for an organization to claim, "We value equity." Instead, equity must be visibly woven into every part of its operations—from hiring practices and budgeting decisions to the way programs are designed and delivered. This approach requires a deliberate effort to ensure that values move beyond words and become active principles that guide daily decisions and behaviors.

- **Codifying Values in Policies:** Ensure every organizational policy explicitly reflects core values.

- **Training and Reinforcement:** Train staff and leadership on operationalizing values in their daily work.

- **Accountability Systems:** Develop metrics to measure whether values are being lived out.

Key Takeaways for Nonprofit COOs

1. **Mission-First Decision-Making:** Every operational decision—from hiring to budget approvals—should support the mission.

2. **Equity in Policy Design:** Policies must balance consistency with compassion, ensuring fairness for all employees, volunteers, and beneficiaries.

3. **Technology as a Servant, Not a Master:** Choose technology tools that support, not control, mission-driven work.

4. **Align People with Purpose:** Recruitment, onboarding, and performance management should always connect staff's work to the broader mission.

5. **Data-Driven Mission Alignment:** Use data to measure how well operations are supporting the mission—and be willing to adapt based on what the data reveals.

Grounding every operational choice in a nonprofit's mission is not just a strategic move—it's a transformational one. When COOs prioritize the mission as the guiding principle behind every decision, they create organizations that are more resilient, impactful, and purpose-driven. This alignment ensures that every dollar spent, every hire made, and every project launched directly supports the organization's ultimate purpose. Instead of operating reactively or chasing short-term gains, mission-driven operations create a cohesive strategy where every action contributes to the larger goal.

Consider the power of this approach: When financial resources are allocated through the lens of the mission, nonprofits avoid wasteful expenditures and focus on high-impact initiatives. Staffing decisions become about more than filling roles—they're about finding people whose personal values and professional skills align with the organization's purpose. Every project—whether it's a fundraising campaign or a community outreach program—becomes a reflection of the mission's heart and soul.

For COOs, this approach demands constant reflection and intentionality. They must ask, "How does this decision serve our mission?" and "Does this process honor our core values?" By embedding these questions into their daily work, COOs position their organizations for long-term growth, sustainable impact, and stronger community trust. Ultimately, mission-driven operations don't just move the needle—they redefine what's possible for the entire nonprofit sector.

.

Part 2: Operational Core Components

Chapter 5: Change Management and Organizational Culture - Leading with Empathy and Clarity

Change is a constant in the nonprofit sector, touching every aspect of an organization's operations. From adopting new tools and technologies to navigating shifting political landscapes and managing organizational growth, nonprofits must continually adapt to maintain relevance and achieve their mission. However, change is rarely straightforward. It's a process that requires strategic foresight, clear communication, and a commitment to the people involved.

For Chief Operating Officers (COOs) and nonprofit leaders, change management goes beyond task lists and implementation schedules. It's about balancing strategic execution with empathy. Successful leaders understand that change impacts people first and processes second. By prioritizing empathy, leaders can anticipate resistance, address concerns, and foster a culture where employees feel supported rather than sidelined.

Leading with empathy means recognizing that change introduces uncertainty, and with uncertainty comes a range of emotions—anxiety, fear, hope, and even excitement. Leaders who acknowledge these emotions and create space for dialogue are better positioned to maintain morale and engagement throughout the change process. This approach helps to shift the organizational mindset from "change is something to fear" to "change is something we do together."

When done well, change management can transform an organization's culture, making it more resilient, agile, and adaptable. It's not just about surviving transitions—it's about using them as opportunities for growth and evolution. Leaders who bridge strategy with empathy ensure their organizations thrive through transformation, strengthening both their internal teams and their ability to achieve their broader mission.

Change isn't just about implementing new systems or processes—it's about guiding people through transitions in a way that strengthens organizational culture and trust. For nonprofits, where staff and stakeholders are often deeply connected to the mission, how change is handled can profoundly affect morale, engagement, and overall effectiveness.

Understanding Organizational Culture

Organizational culture represents the shared values, beliefs, and behaviors that define how an organization operates. In nonprofits, culture is often deeply tied to the mission, creating a sense of purpose that drives both staff and stakeholders. A strong culture acts as a compass during times of change, providing stability and clarity in decision-making and communication.

To navigate change effectively, it's essential to understand the different types of organizational culture and how they influence an organization's ability to adapt. Research identifies four primary types: Clan, Hierarchy, Market, and Adhocracy. Each type offers unique strengths and challenges, but nonprofits typically thrive in a Clan Culture, which prioritizes collaboration, trust, and shared values.

This section draws upon concepts from Cameron and Quinn's *"Diagnosing and Changing Organizational Culture"* (2006), which outlines the Competing Values Framework as a foundational approach to understanding organizational culture.

The Four Types of Organizational Culture

1. **Clan Culture**
   Key Characteristics: Collaboration, teamwork, trust, and shared values.
   Strengths: Focuses on people, fostering loyalty and engagement. Thrives in environments where a sense of community and belonging is essential.
   Challenges: Can struggle with decision-making speed and accountability if not balanced with clear structures.

2. **Hierarchy Culture**
   Key Characteristics: Formal processes, clear roles, and structured decision-making.
   Strengths: Ensures consistency and efficiency, particularly in compliance-heavy environments.
   Challenges: Can stifle creativity and adaptability, leading to resistance to change.

3. **Market Culture**

   Key Characteristics: Results-oriented, competitive, and driven by external success metrics.

   Strengths: Encourages innovation and a focus on measurable outcomes.

   Challenges: May overlook internal cohesion and long-term mission alignment.

4. **Adhocracy Culture**

   Key Characteristics: Flexibility, creativity, and a focus on innovation.

   Strengths: Excels in dynamic environments where adaptability and risk-taking are critical.

   Challenges: Can lack stability and clear direction, creating confusion in mission-focused work.

Why Nonprofits Thrive in a Clan Culture

Nonprofits often operate in environments where collaboration and shared values are paramount. Unlike for-profit organizations that may prioritize competition or market-driven objectives, nonprofits are mission-driven at their core. This mission-driven approach attracts people who are deeply committed to the cause, and this commitment extends beyond their job descriptions. Staff and stakeholders form a community bound by shared purpose and a collective desire to make a positive impact.

At the heart of this community is a Clan Culture, a model of organizational culture characterized by its emphasis on teamwork, trust, and shared ownership of the mission.

Clan Culture fosters an environment where people feel connected not just to their work but to each other. This interconnectedness creates a sense of belonging and a personal investment in the organization's success. Leaders play a vital role in nurturing this culture by promoting open communication, recognizing contributions, and fostering relationships across all levels of the organization.

One illustrative example of Clan Culture in action is seen in how organizations handle significant transitions, such as the adoption of new technology. During Faith in Public Life's transition to Asana for project management, the principles of Clan Culture were at the forefront. The leadership team approached the change with intentionality, prioritizing values like clarity, transparency, and collaboration. By involving staff in the decision-making process and maintaining open channels for feedback, they ensured that the transition was not just a shift in tools but an affirmation of their collective mission. This process not only improved operational efficiency but also reinforced the organization's mission-driven culture, leaving staff feeling more connected and invested in the outcome.

In essence, Clan Culture is not just a "nice to have" for nonprofits—it is a strategic asset. It fuels morale, promotes psychological safety, and creates a work environment where people feel empowered to contribute their best efforts. When people feel a deep sense of belonging, they are more resilient in the face of change, more willing to collaborate, and more committed to achieving the organization's mission.

The Nonprofit Change Curve

Change often follows a predictable pattern of emotional and psychological responses, outlined in the Change Curve model:

1. **Shock and Denial:** Resistance or disbelief about the need for change.

2. **Frustration and Resistance:** Pushback as people begin to grapple with new realities.

3. **Exploration and Experimentation:** Openness to trying new approaches.

4. **Acceptance and Integration:** Full adoption of the change as part of everyday operations.

The Change Curve model draws on foundational insights from Elizabeth Kubler-Ross's *"Five Stages of Grief"* framework, adapted to the context of organizational change management.

At FPL, staff moved through these stages during the rollout of Asana. Initially, there was skepticism about whether a new tool was necessary. Some team members feared it would complicate workflows rather than streamline them. Recognizing these concerns, leadership guided the organization through the curve by:

- **Acknowledging Resistance:** Creating spaces where staff could voice their concerns.

- **Providing Training and Resources:** Bringing in an external organization to deliver project management training, ensuring staff felt supported.

- **Highlighting Early Wins**: Demonstrating how Asana simplified cross-departmental collaboration through shared task tracking and timelines.

By embracing the Change Curve, FPL not only implemented Asana successfully but also fostered a culture of openness and adaptability.

The Role of Empathy in Change Management

Empathy is one of the most powerful tools in a COO's arsenal, serving as a bridge between leadership decisions and the human experience of change. When employees feel heard, respected, and supported during times of transformation, they are more likely to engage with the process, overcome resistance, and embrace new ways of working. Empathy is not about avoiding tough decisions— it's about approaching those decisions with compassion and clarity.

Effective empathetic leadership begins with active listening. Leaders must create dedicated spaces where staff can voice their concerns, ask questions, and share their perspectives. Whether through one-on-one conversations, town hall meetings, or anonymous feedback channels, these opportunities for dialogue demonstrate that leadership values employee input.

Transparency is another essential element of empathy in change management. When leaders clearly communicate the reasons behind a change, the expected impact, and the steps being taken to support staff, they reduce fear and uncertainty. Transparent messaging reinforces trust and helps staff feel more secure, even in times of upheaval.

Moreover, empathetic leaders recognize that change affects people differently. Some may adapt quickly, while others require more time and support. Providing tailored resources—like training sessions, job aids, and one-on-one coaching—demonstrates a commitment to individual well-being. Empathy in change management is not a "one-size-fits-all" approach but a customized strategy that addresses the unique needs of each person and team.

Finally, leaders must model empathy through their actions. This means acknowledging the emotional toll of change, showing patience when setbacks occur, and celebrating small victories along the way. By doing so, leaders create a sense of psychological safety, where employees feel confident taking risks, asking for help, and ultimately embracing the change.

In my time at FPL, we encountered this need for empathy when developing the Standard Operating Procedure (SOP) for using Salesforce and Asana. For many staff, the introduction of these tools represented a significant shift in how they approached relationship management and project planning. By actively engaging staff during the SOP development process, we ensured their input shaped the final document. This approach not only eased anxieties but also created a sense of ownership among team members.

Practical Strategies for Managing Change

1. **Start with a Clear Vision**: Clearly articulate the purpose of the change and how it aligns with the organization's mission.

2. **Engage Stakeholders Early**: Involve staff, board members, and other stakeholders in the planning process to build buy-in and address potential concerns.

3. **Develop a Transition Plan**: Create a step-by-step roadmap for implementing the change, including timelines, responsibilities, and milestones.

4. **Provide Training and Resources**: Equip staff with the tools and knowledge they need to succeed in the new environment.

5. **Communicate Consistently**: Use multiple channels to keep stakeholders informed, addressing questions and providing updates throughout the process.

6. **Monitor Progress and Adjust**: Regularly assess how the change is being implemented and make adjustments based on feedback and results.

Building Resilience for Future Change

Change management is not merely about navigating immediate transitions; it's a philosophy that positions change as an ever-present force for growth and transformation. Successful change leaders understand that every shift—whether a new software implementation, a strategic pivot, or a shift in stakeholder expectations— can be an opportunity to strengthen the organization's cultural fabric. Embracing this approach requires foresight, patience, and an unwavering commitment to shared values.

Rather than viewing change as a disruption, forward-thinking organizations see it as a catalyst for innovation and adaptability. This mindset shift begins with proactive planning, which involves anticipating future changes and preparing the organization's people, processes, and resources. Leaders must create structured pathways for change, ensuring that every transition is supported by clear objectives, a strategic roadmap, and achievable milestones.

Ongoing professional development plays a vital role in this process. By equipping staff with new skills and fostering a culture of continuous learning, organizations can build a workforce that is agile and ready to face the challenges of the unknown. Training sessions, mentorship opportunities, and peer-to-peer learning experiences all contribute to this goal, ensuring that employees feel supported rather than threatened by the shifts they encounter.

Collaboration sits at the heart of resilient change management. No leader can execute change alone. By bringing together diverse voices from across the organization—staff, board members, and external stakeholders—leaders can create an inclusive change process that builds collective ownership. When employees see that their perspectives are valued and integrated into the change process, they're more likely to remain engaged, committed, and adaptable as the organization evolves.

At OKCNP, for example, we integrated change management into our leadership training programs. By equipping nonprofit leaders with the tools to navigate transitions, we helped build a culture of resilience across the sector. Similarly, at FPL, the successful implementation of Asana laid the groundwork for future operational improvements, demonstrating the power of strategic and empathetic change management.

Key Takeaways for Nonprofit Leaders

- Organizational culture is a foundation for managing change. Align transitions with shared values and mission.

- The Change Curve provides insight into how people respond to transitions, helping leaders tailor their approach.

- Empathy and transparency are essential for addressing concerns and building trust during change.

- Practical strategies, from training to consistent communication, can facilitate successful transitions.

- Building resilience requires a proactive approach to planning and professional development.

Chapter 6: Financial Oversight - Budgeting, Cash Flow, and Ethical Stewardship

Fundamentals of Nonprofit Financial Management

Financial oversight is a foundational pillar of nonprofit operations, shaping decisions that range from program expansion to staffing capacity. While it's often perceived as a technical exercise centered on managing spreadsheets, audits, and financial statements, its true essence lies in stewardship. At its core, financial oversight is about aligning resources with impact, fostering transparency, and reinforcing trust with funders, stakeholders, and the broader community. It's a dynamic process that ensures every financial decision upholds the integrity and mission of the organization. Through thoughtful oversight, nonprofit leaders demonstrate their commitment to responsible resource management, thereby enhancing organizational credibility and securing sustainable growth.

Unlike for-profit entities, nonprofits face unique financial challenges, such as unpredictable revenue streams, funder restrictions, and the need to balance short-term needs with long-term sustainability. This chapter explores how nonprofit leaders, especially Chief Operating Officers (COOs) and finance committees, can build a solid financial foundation, align financial practices with the organization's mission, and prepare for potential financial crises.

Budgeting Process and Cash Flow Management

A well-planned budget serves as a financial roadmap, providing a clear path that aligns resources with strategic priorities and organizational goals. It is not merely a numerical exercise; it is a dynamic tool that reflects the mission and values of the organization. Effective budgeting requires nonprofit leaders to approach the process with clarity, collaboration, and adaptability. Clarity ensures all stakeholders have a shared understanding of financial priorities. Collaboration invites input from program directors, department leads, and board members, fostering a sense of ownership and shared responsibility. Adaptability is essential to account for changes in the funding landscape, unexpected expenses, or emerging opportunities. Together, these principles create a budgeting process that is both strategic and flexible, enabling nonprofits to remain mission-focused even in the face of financial uncertainty.

1. The Budgeting Process

- **Start Early and Plan Collaboratively**: Budgeting should begin months before the start of the fiscal year. Engage program directors, department leads, and board members to ensure alignment with organizational goals. Early planning provides room for adjustments and consensus-building.

- **Use a Zero-Based Approach**: For specific initiatives, consider zero-based budgeting, where every expense must be justified from scratch. This approach helps avoid wasteful spending and ensures every dollar is purposefully allocated.

- **Incorporate Strategic Priorities**: Budgets should reflect the organization's mission and strategic goals. For example, if equity and advocacy are core values, the budget should prioritize funding for related activities, even if that means cutting costs elsewhere.

- **Build Flexibility into the Budget**: Set aside contingency funds to cover unexpected expenses. This ensures that the organization can respond to sudden changes in the financial landscape, such as economic downturns or emergency funding needs.

2. Budget Implementation and Monitoring

- **Approval and Rollout**: After board approval, share the final budget with key stakeholders. Ensure department heads understand their spending limits and financial responsibilities.

- **Track Expenditures in Real Time**: Use accounting software to track expenses against the approved budget. Regular monitoring allows for timely adjustments and prevents over-expenditure.

- **Conduct Mid-Year Reviews**: Midway through the fiscal year, review financial performance. Identify areas where spending exceeds the budget and address potential shortfalls. This review period is crucial for ensuring accountability and maintaining financial health.

3. Cash Flow Management

- **Forecast Cash Flow**: Cash flow is distinct from budget planning. It focuses on the timing of income and expenses. Create cash flow projections to identify when cash will be tight and plan accordingly.

- **Diversify Revenue Streams**: Relying on a single funding source is risky. Diversify revenue through grants, donations, and earned income to maintain liquidity.

- **Maintain Operating Reserves**: Aim to maintain 3-6 months of operating expenses in an unrestricted reserve fund. This "safety net" provides stability during cash flow gaps.

Ethical Stewardship of Funds and Donor Expectations

Ethical stewardship extends well beyond compliance; it is a profound commitment to upholding the trust that donors, funders, and stakeholders place in the organization. It's about ensuring that every financial decision, from the acceptance of donations to the allocation of resources, reflects the organization's mission, values, and ethical principles. Ethical stewardship demands transparency, accountability, and deliberate decision-making, recognizing that each dollar entrusted to the organization carries with it the weight of donor intent and community impact. Here's how nonprofit leaders can establish and maintain ethical financial management in their organizations:

1. Transparency and Accountability

- **Clear Reporting**: Share financial updates with the board, funders, and staff. Regularly provide clear financial statements, including income statements, balance sheets, and cash flow reports.

- **Use Dashboards**: Create dashboards that display key financial metrics, such as cash on hand, program spending, and donor contributions. Visual dashboards make it easier for board members to understand the financial picture.

- **Host Finance Meetings**: Hold monthly or quarterly finance meetings with program leads to review spending. This promotes transparency and accountability at all levels of the organization.

2. Ethical Fundraising and Gift Acceptance

- **Gift Acceptance Policies**: Not all donations are "good" donations. Have a gift acceptance policy that outlines the types of gifts the organization can accept. Declining gifts that come with problematic stipulations protects the organization's mission and integrity.

- **Donor Stewardship**: Recognize and thank donors promptly. Transparency with donors about how their funds are used builds trust and encourages future giving.

- **Avoid Misuse of Funds**: Ensure that restricted funds (funds earmarked for specific purposes) are used as intended. Mismanagement of restricted funds can lead to reputational damage and legal consequences.

3. Financial Controls and Internal Checks

- **Segregation of Duties**: Separate financial responsibilities to prevent fraud. For example, one person collects cash donations, another deposits them, and a third person reconciles the accounts.

- **Expense Reimbursement Policies**: Set clear guidelines for reimbursable expenses and require original receipts. Define timelines for submission and review to avoid confusion.

- **Audit and Compliance**: Conduct annual financial audits by a third-party auditor. Internal audits should also be performed periodically to identify potential issues early.

Preparing for Financial Crises

Financial crises can strike nonprofits unexpectedly, stemming from factors such as economic downturns, shifts in funder priorities, or the sudden loss of key donors. These events have the potential to destabilize even the most financially sound organizations. However, with thoughtful preparation and proactive planning, nonprofits can significantly mitigate the impact of such crises. By identifying potential risks, maintaining emergency reserves, and developing contingency plans, organizations can navigate financial disruptions with resilience. Preparing for crises also involves fostering a culture of financial agility, where staff and leadership are equipped to make timely, informed decisions under pressure. Through these measures, nonprofits can protect their mission-critical programs and maintain the trust of stakeholders, even in the face of financial adversity.

1. Risk Management and Contingency Planning

- **Identify Vulnerabilities**: Use a risk assessment matrix to identify potential threats, such as loss of grant funding or increased operational costs.

- **Scenario Planning**: Develop contingency plans for worst-case scenarios. For instance, plan how to operate with a 10% revenue loss.

- **Emergency Reserves**: Maintain an emergency reserve fund to cover at least 3-6 months of operating expenses.

2. Crisis Response

- **Activate Emergency Protocols**: When a financial crisis occurs, activate an emergency response plan. This may involve freezing non-essential spending or pivoting fundraising strategies.

- **Prioritize Core Functions**: Focus on essential operations. Identify which programs must continue and which can be paused or scaled back.

- **Communicate Transparently**: Keep stakeholders informed about the crisis and the organization's response. Transparency maintains trust and can inspire emergency donations.

Key Takeaways

1. **Budgeting and Cash Flow**: Plan early, engage stakeholders, and build flexibility into the budget. Cash flow forecasts ensure liquidity, while reserves protect against financial shocks.

2. **Ethical Stewardship**: Ethical management builds donor trust and preserves the organization's reputation. Transparency, donor stewardship, and gift acceptance policies are essential.

3. **Financial Controls**: Segregate duties, establish strong internal controls, and conduct audits to reduce the risk of fraud or mismanagement.

4. **Crisis Preparedness**: Proactive planning reduces the impact of financial crises. Scenario planning, emergency reserves, and timely communication ensure resilience.

Mastering financial oversight requires more than technical skills—it demands integrity, strategic foresight, and the ability to adapt to ever-evolving challenges. This role extends beyond managing numbers on a page; it requires nonprofit leaders to act as stewards of public trust, ensuring that every financial decision serves the mission of the organization. By embedding these practices into daily operations, nonprofit leaders cultivate a culture of financial responsibility, transparency, and accountability. Such a culture not only safeguards the organization's current stability but also builds its capacity for long-term growth and impact. Leaders who prioritize ethical oversight are better positioned to navigate economic uncertainty, sustain donor confidence, and drive strategic initiatives forward.

.

Chapter 7: Policy and Compliance - How to Build an Ethical and Accountable Operation

Introduction Policies and compliance are the backbone of ethical and effective nonprofit operations. They create a shared understanding of organizational expectations, protect mission integrity, and ensure compliance with legal, regulatory, and financial standards. For Chief Operating Officers (COOs) and nonprofit leaders, mastering the development and implementation of these policies is one of the most impactful ways to sustain operational excellence and build stakeholder trust.

This chapter provides a comprehensive guide to essential nonprofit policies, including how to create, revise, and implement them. We'll also highlight the Standards for Excellence® framework as a tool for enhancing operational integrity. You'll find actionable insights and practical guidance for building an ethical and accountable nonprofit.

Core Policies Every Nonprofit Must Have A well-constructed policy framework serves as the cornerstone of effective nonprofit governance and operational excellence. These policies do more than set rules—they provide a clear path for decision-making, risk management, and the alignment of actions with the organization's mission. For nonprofit leaders, having a comprehensive suite of essential policies establishes consistency, promotes accountability, and ensures compliance with legal and regulatory standards. Each policy serves a distinct role in safeguarding the organization's integrity, supporting its operational needs, and enhancing its capacity to deliver on its mission. Below is an overview of the essential policies that every nonprofit should develop and implement to build a strong, ethical, and effective operational foundation:

1. **Governance Policies**

   o **Bylaws:** Define the organization's legal structure, mission, and operational rules. Bylaws set the ground rules for decision-making, board composition, and member responsibilities.

   o **Conflict of Interest Policy:** Ensures decisions are made in the best interest of the nonprofit, free from personal gain. This policy requires disclosures of conflicts and outlines procedures for managing them.

   o **Whistleblower Protection Policy:** Protects employees and stakeholders who report unethical or illegal behavior. It outlines reporting procedures and assures protection against retaliation.

   o **Board Recruitment Policy:** Establishes clear guidelines for identifying, recruiting, and onboarding new board members, ensuring a diverse and skilled board.

2. **Operational Policies**

- ○ **Technology Use Policy:** Defines how staff can use organizational technology and outlines cybersecurity measures to protect sensitive data.

- ○ **Document Retention Policy:** Establishes how long key documents are retained and how they are destroyed once no longer needed. This policy ensures legal compliance and operational efficiency.

- ○ **Risk Management Policy:** Identifies potential risks and outlines strategies to mitigate them. This includes risk assessments for financial, operational, and reputational risks.

- ○ **Safety and Security Policy:** Outlines emergency procedures for evacuations, shelter-in-place protocols, and cybersecurity protocols to protect staff and organizational assets.

3. **Financial Policies**

- ○ **Budgeting Policy:** Provides guidelines for creating, reviewing, and approving the organization's annual budget to ensure alignment with strategic goals.

- ○ **Expense Reimbursement Policy:** Details the process for reimbursing employee expenses, ensuring fairness, consistency, and compliance with IRS regulations.

- ○ **Gift Acceptance Policy:** Outlines what types of gifts the nonprofit will accept and under what conditions. It ensures that gifts align with the organization's mission and do not pose undue burdens or conflicts.

- ○ **Investment Policy:** Establishes guidelines for how the organization's financial reserves will be managed, invested, and reviewed to ensure mission-aligned stewardship.

4. **HR and Personnel Policies**

- ○ **Employee Handbook:** The central document outlining workplace policies, rights, and responsibilities. It includes leave policies, performance management, and discipline procedures.

- ○ **Anti-Harassment and Anti-Discrimination Policy:** Prohibits harassment and discrimination in the workplace and outlines procedures for reporting, investigating, and resolving complaints.

- ○ **Remote Work Policy:** Establishes the criteria for remote work eligibility, communication expectations, and technology use requirements.

How to Create and Revise Policies Crafting and revising nonprofit policies is a dynamic process that requires transparency, inclusivity, and continuous improvement. A well-thought-out approach ensures that policies remain relevant, practical, and aligned with the organization's mission and values. Here's a detailed, step-by-step approach to guide nonprofit leaders through this essential process:

1. **Identify Organizational Needs**

   o   Conduct a gap analysis to determine which policies are missing or outdated.

   o   Prioritize policies based on legal, operational, and strategic needs.

2. **Research and Benchmark**

   o   Review sample policies from trusted sources, such as the Standards for Excellence® or nonprofit associations.

   o   Align policy content with applicable federal, state, and local laws, as well as industry best practices.

3. **Draft the Policy**

   o   Use clear, concise language that can be understood by all stakeholders.

   o   Include key sections such as purpose, scope, roles, procedures, and review dates.

4. **Engage Stakeholders**

   o   Involve board members, leadership, and staff in the policy review process.

- Solicit feedback to ensure buy-in and practicality in daily operations.

5. **Obtain Board Approval**

   - Submit the draft policy for review and approval by the board or a relevant committee.

   - Ensure that the policy aligns with the organization's mission and legal obligations.

6. **Implement and Train**

   - Distribute the policy to all relevant stakeholders.

   - Provide training to ensure staff understand the policy's purpose and their responsibilities.

7. **Review and Update**

   - Schedule periodic reviews (e.g., annually or every three years) to ensure relevance and compliance.

   - Document any revisions and communicate them to all stakeholders.

For a more detailed exploration of essential policies and best practices, refer to *Policies and Procedures for Nonprofit Success: A Comprehensive Guide to Ethical and Effective Governance*. This resource delves deeper into policy templates, operational guidance, and the legal rationale for key policies.

Real-World Case Studies

1. **Case Study: Progressive Discipline Policy**

    o **Challenge:** FPL faced inconsistencies in how employee performance issues were handled, leading to confusion and frustration among staff.

    o **Solution:** FPL developed a clear Progressive Discipline Policy outlining coaching, verbal and written warnings, performance improvement plans (PIPs), and potential termination.

    o **Impact:** The policy provided clarity, fairness, and consistency, leading to more effective management of employee performance issues.

2. **Case Study: Safety and Security Policy**

    o **Challenge:** Political activism and potential threats required clear protocols for staff safety at FPL.

    o **Solution:** FPL implemented a Safety and Security Policy covering emergency evacuations, cybersecurity, and travel safety measures.

- ○ **Impact:** Staff felt more secure knowing there were clear procedures to follow in emergencies, and the organization's liability was reduced.

Key Takeaways for COOs and Nonprofit Leaders

1. **Prioritize Mission Alignment:** Policies should reinforce the mission, values, and ethical principles of the organization.

2. **Engage Stakeholders:** Staff, board members, and stakeholders should be involved in policy development and revisions.

3. **Use Clear Language:** Avoid legal jargon and create policies that are accessible to all staff and volunteers.

4. **Review and Update:** Schedule regular reviews of key policies to ensure they remain relevant and compliant.

5. **Leverage Existing Resources:** Use the *Policies and Procedures for Nonprofit Success* guide as a reference for policy templates, tools, and implementation tips.

By building a robust framework of ethical policies and compliance protocols, nonprofits can foster trust, transparency, and operational integrity. This not only enhances internal efficiency but also builds credibility with funders, regulators, and the communities they serve.

Chapter 8: Technology and Cybersecurity - Protecting Your Mission in a Digital World

Technology has become an indispensable part of nonprofit operations, weaving its way into every facet of an organization's activities. From managing donor relationships and streamlining internal communication to facilitating program delivery, technology plays a pivotal role in boosting efficiency, enhancing transparency, and amplifying overall impact. However, with greater reliance on technology comes an increased exposure to potential risks. Cybersecurity threats, such as phishing attacks and ransomware, as well as data breaches and system failures, have the potential to disrupt operations and erode stakeholder trust. This evolving digital landscape demands that nonprofit leaders adopt a proactive approach, balancing technological advancement with robust cybersecurity measures to protect their mission and ensure operational continuity.

For nonprofit COOs, the challenge is twofold: adopting the right tools to power your mission while protecting against cybersecurity threats. This chapter offers a roadmap for nonprofit leaders to leverage technology securely and effectively.

Key Operational Tools for Efficiency and Security

1. CRM (Constituent Relationship Management) Systems

CRMs are the backbone of donor engagement and relationship management. Systems like Salesforce, Bloomerang, and DonorPerfect allow nonprofits to track donor interactions, manage gift records, and cultivate relationships over time.

Best Practices:

- Choose a CRM that integrates with your existing tools (like Asana or Google Workspace).

- Ensure role-based access to protect donor data.

- Regularly audit user permissions.

2. Donor Management Software

Donor management software is often a core feature of CRMs but can also be standalone platforms. These tools enhance donor cultivation, process donations, and provide donor analytics.

Best Practices:

- Implement multi-factor authentication (MFA) to secure login access.

- Encrypt donor information during transmission and storage.

- Regularly review data storage practices for GDPR and other compliance standards.

3. Project Management Systems

Tools like Asana, Trello, and Monday.com help nonprofits manage workflows, assign tasks, and maintain visibility on project status. FPL's adoption of Asana, for instance, streamlined cross-departmental collaboration, improving efficiency and accountability.

Best Practices:

- Clearly define project roles and responsibilities.

- Use Asana's permissions to restrict access to sensitive tasks.

- Train staff on how to use collaboration features to avoid information silos.

Cybersecurity Best Practices for Nonprofits

As nonprofits continue to expand their reliance on digital tools, the need for robust cybersecurity measures becomes increasingly urgent. Every digital interaction, from processing donor information to managing internal communications, presents a potential vulnerability. Without proper safeguards, nonprofits risk exposing sensitive financial information, donor data, and operational details to cybercriminals. The fallout from a cybersecurity breach can be severe, including financial loss, reputational damage, and erosion of stakeholder trust. Preventative measures are not just an option but a necessity for organizations aiming to maintain operational integrity and uphold the confidence of donors, staff, and beneficiaries. By adopting a proactive cybersecurity strategy, nonprofits can fortify their defenses, reduce risk, and protect the core of their mission-driven work.

1. Develop a Cybersecurity Policy

A written cybersecurity policy defines protocols for system access, password management, software updates, and incident response.

Key Elements:

- Role-based access control: Staff only access information essential to their role.

- Password guidelines: Use strong passwords and require changes periodically.

- Incident response plan: Detail what steps to take in the event of a breach.

2. Staff Training and Awareness

Staff errors are a leading cause of data breaches. Training ensures employees recognize phishing scams, avoid unsecured networks, and follow secure data practices.

Training Priorities:

- Identify phishing attempts and social engineering attacks.

- Protect sensitive data during remote work (e.g., use VPNs).

- Recognize and report suspicious system behavior.

3. Use Multi-Factor Authentication (MFA)

MFA requires users to verify their identity using two or more methods before accessing systems, making it harder for hackers to compromise accounts.

Implementation Tips:

- Enable MFA for CRM, email, and financial management systems.

- Use authentication apps like Google Authenticator or Microsoft Authenticator.

4. Data Backup and Recovery

Regular backups ensure that your organization's information can be restored in case of a system failure, breach, or ransomware attack.

Best Practices:

- Use both on-site and cloud-based backups.

- Test data recovery procedures quarterly to ensure backups are functional.

5. Limit Access to Critical Systems

Role-based access control (RBAC) limits the information staff can access, reducing the impact of a breach.

Steps to Implement:

- Use "least privilege" principles—give staff access only to what's needed for their role.

- Review access logs periodically to identify unusual access patterns.

6. Conduct Regular Cybersecurity Audits

Routine audits assess the strength of cybersecurity measures and identify vulnerabilities.

What to Include in an Audit:

- Penetration testing: Test your systems' ability to withstand cyberattacks.

- Compliance checks: Ensure alignment with GDPR, HIPAA, or other applicable regulations.

- Vulnerability scans: Use automated tools to identify security gaps.

Integrating Technology into Organizational Culture

Technology adoption is not just about selecting and implementing software—it's about fostering a culture where staff understand, trust, and effectively use technology as part of their daily workflows. This requires more than a one-time orientation. It calls for ongoing training, the use of intuitive, user-friendly tools, and the establishment of clear, accessible protocols that guide employees in using technology securely and efficiently. By nurturing this culture, nonprofits can increase staff confidence in digital tools, reduce resistance to change, and ensure that technology adoption leads to meaningful improvements in productivity, collaboration, and mission impact. An engaged, tech-savvy workforce becomes an asset, driving operational excellence and mitigating risks associated with improper tool usage or security vulnerabilities.

Strategies for Building a Tech-Savvy Culture:

- **Onboard with Care:** Provide new staff with training on key tools and security protocols.

- **Recognize Early Adopters:** Highlight staff who embrace and promote tech adoption.

- **Assign a Tech Champion:** This person serves as a go-to resource for staff questions.

Technology on a Budget

Many nonprofits face financial constraints, but tight budgets shouldn't be a barrier to accessing essential technology. While large organizations may have the resources to invest in cutting-edge tools, smaller nonprofits can still thrive by being resourceful, strategic, and informed about available options. Embracing technology on a budget requires creativity and a clear understanding of the tools that offer the most impact for the least cost. Here's how to make the most of your tech investments:

1. Leverage Nonprofit Discounts Many providers offer discounted rates for nonprofits, including Microsoft, Adobe, and Google.

2. Use Open-Source Tools Platforms like LibreOffice (an alternative to Microsoft Office) offer free, open-source alternatives to costly software.

3. Prioritize Must-Have Features Focus on software that solves multiple issues. For example, Asana combines project management, collaboration, and task tracking.

4. Apply for Technology Grants Grants specifically for technology adoption are available from foundations like TechSoup, Google for Nonprofits, and the Nonprofit Technology Enterprise Network (NTEN).

Preparing for Future Tech Needs

Technology is constantly evolving, and nonprofits must prepare for this evolution to remain agile, innovative, and resilient. Staying ahead of technological shifts requires strategic foresight, regular review of emerging trends, and a commitment to continuous learning. Nonprofits that anticipate changes in technology can adapt their operations, leverage new tools for increased efficiency, and protect their organizations from potential disruptions. This proactive approach ensures that nonprofits remain relevant, mission-focused, and ready to seize opportunities for growth. By embracing future-ready strategies, nonprofit leaders can foster an environment where technology becomes a catalyst for mission advancement rather than a source of uncertainty.

How to Stay Ahead:

1. **Trend Monitoring:** In a rapidly changing digital landscape, staying ahead of industry trends is essential for nonprofit leaders. Keeping an eye on emerging tools, platforms, and technological

advancements allows organizations to remain agile and responsive. This proactive approach helps nonprofits anticipate shifts that could impact operations, fundraising, and program delivery. Regularly engaging with industry reports, attending tech conferences, and networking with other nonprofit leaders can provide valuable insights. By staying informed, nonprofit leaders are better positioned to adopt transformative tools early, optimize efficiency, and maintain a competitive edge in achieving their mission.

2. **Budget for Upgrades:** Ensuring your nonprofit remains technologically current requires dedicated financial planning. By including tech upgrades as a specific line item in the annual budget, organizations can proactively address software updates, hardware replacements, and the adoption of new tools. This approach avoids the financial strain of unexpected tech needs and supports strategic growth. Setting aside a dedicated budget for upgrades demonstrates a commitment to innovation, operational efficiency, and cybersecurity resilience. By planning for these costs annually, nonprofits can avoid reactive spending and maintain a steady, predictable path toward technological advancement.

3. **Invest in Training:** Continuous learning is essential for ensuring that staff remain adept at using the latest software and technological tools. By providing ongoing access to training opportunities,

nonprofits empower their teams to adapt to system updates, new features, and emerging best practices. This approach not only boosts operational efficiency but also fosters a culture of continuous improvement. Training sessions can be delivered in various formats, such as live workshops, on-demand webinars, or self-paced online courses. When staff are confident in their ability to use new tools effectively, they become more engaged, productive, and better equipped to contribute to the nonprofit's mission. Moreover, skilled employees are less likely to encounter technical errors, which reduces support requests and operational disruptions.

Key Takeaways for Nonprofit COOs

- **Invest in Cybersecurity:** Protection against data breaches is as critical as operational efficiency.

- **Adopt Scalable Tools:** Choose software that grows with your nonprofit.

- **Build a Culture of Tech Competency:** Training, support, and recognition ensure smooth adoption.

- **Budget for Tech Growth:** Use grants, discounts, and smart planning to stretch your tech dollars.

By thoughtfully selecting and safeguarding technology, nonprofit COOs hold the power to revolutionize their organization's operations. This careful approach enables them to streamline workflows, enhance cross-departmental collaboration, and achieve mission-critical objectives with greater efficiency. Additionally, by prioritizing data protection and implementing robust cybersecurity measures, COOs can safeguard sensitive stakeholder information, uphold donor trust, and mitigate the risk of breaches. Such forward-thinking leadership not only fortifies the nonprofit's resilience against external threats but also positions the organization as a model of operational excellence in the mission-driven sector.

Part 3: People and Talent Management

Chapter 9: Employee Engagement, Professional Development, and Onboarding

Employee Lifecycle in Nonprofits

The employee lifecycle in nonprofits represents the entire journey of an employee's experience with the organization, from the first point of contact during recruitment to their eventual departure. Each stage of this journey offers unique opportunities to reinforce the organization's mission, foster growth, and strengthen employee engagement. By approaching this lifecycle with intentionality, nonprofit COOs can create a workplace culture that inspires commitment, purpose, and excellence.

Recruitment

Recruitment is the foundation of the employee lifecycle. It's the process of attracting and selecting candidates whose skills, values, and ambitions align with the mission of the organization. While recruitment is often viewed as simply filling vacancies, it's much more than that. It's about identifying and engaging people who see themselves as part of the organization's long-term story. This process includes crafting compelling job descriptions, using strategic outreach methods, and ensuring the candidate experience is welcoming, inclusive, and clear about expectations. When recruitment is done well, it increases the likelihood of long-term employee satisfaction and retention.

Onboarding

Onboarding is where new employees are introduced to the organization's culture, mission, and operational systems. The goal is to ensure that new hires feel welcomed, prepared, and supported as they transition into their roles. A comprehensive onboarding process includes pre-onboarding activities like welcome emails and access to key resources, as well as first-day experiences where new hires meet their teams, receive technology access, and review important organizational policies. Structured onboarding plans often include a 30-, 60-, and 90-day roadmap to ensure employees are steadily growing in their knowledge, skills, and confidence.

Development

Employee development ensures that staff continue to grow and evolve alongside the needs of the organization. Continuous learning opportunities, like workshops, certifications, and leadership development programs, demonstrate the organization's investment in its employees. Developmental experiences keep employees engaged, build new skills, and prepare them for expanded roles and responsibilities. By prioritizing development, organizations strengthen their internal talent pipeline and reduce turnover caused by stagnation or dissatisfaction.

Retention

Retention is the act of keeping employees engaged and committed to the organization's mission. High retention rates signal a healthy organizational culture, while low rates can be a sign of deeper issues. Retention strategies should include competitive compensation, recognition programs, clear pathways for advancement, and consistent communication. Retaining employees also reduces recruitment and training costs, preserves institutional knowledge, and enhances the sense of community within the nonprofit.

Separation

Separation occurs when an employee leaves the organization, either voluntarily or involuntarily. While this can be a challenging experience for both the employee and the organization, it's also an opportunity for learning. Exit interviews offer valuable insights into the employee experience, revealing potential areas of improvement in leadership, culture, or operations. Handling departures with empathy and professionalism ensures that former employees remain advocates for the organization.

Creating an Employee Onboarding Plan

Onboarding is more than a one-day orientation. It's a structured process that sets the tone for an employee's journey within the organization. Nonprofit COOs should develop an onboarding process that promotes belonging, establishes clarity, and accelerates time-to-productivity. Here's a deeper exploration of the essential components of a strong onboarding plan:

Pre-Onboarding: Building Excitement and Connection

Pre-onboarding starts before the employee's first day. The goal is to reduce anxiety and create anticipation. Sending a welcome email that outlines what to expect on day one can go a long way in reducing uncertainty. Sharing organizational values, team introductions, and links to essential documents helps employees feel connected and informed. Assigning a mentor or buddy gives new hires a personal touchpoint, encouraging them to ask questions and seek guidance.

Day One: Making a Strong First Impression

The first day sets the stage for the entire employee experience. It's a time to make employees feel valued and seen. Activities might include a welcome breakfast, a tour of the office (virtual or in-person), and a welcome message from the executive director or senior leadership. This day should be structured but not overwhelming, and it should provide clear guidance on expectations and role-specific responsibilities.

Role-Specific Training: Equipping Employees for Success

Employees need specific skills and knowledge to be successful in their roles. Role-specific training goes beyond general orientation and focuses on the tools, processes, and tasks the employee will use daily. Training plans should have clear milestones at 30, 60, and 90 days. Regular check-ins with supervisors ensure employees feel supported, can ask questions, and can reflect on their progress.

Ongoing Integration: Sustaining Engagement and Momentum

Onboarding doesn't end after 30 or 90 days. Continued support and engagement are crucial. Encourage employees to participate in cross-departmental one-on-ones to broaden their understanding of the organization. Celebrate milestones like 90 days, one-year anniversaries, or the completion of major projects. Feedback from employees during this phase can be used to refine and improve future onboarding experiences.

Review and Refinement

Onboarding processes must be dynamic. Solicit feedback from employees and supervisors to identify areas for improvement. Organizations can track key onboarding metrics, such as time-to-productivity and new hire retention rates, to measure success. As the organization grows, so should its onboarding strategy.

Employee Engagement Strategies

Employee engagement is a multifaceted and ever-evolving process that requires ongoing attention and intentional effort. Unlike a one-time initiative or a static policy, engagement is a continuous cycle that demands thoughtful leadership, open communication, and a genuine commitment to employee well-being. For nonprofit COOs, fostering engagement is about more than maintaining productivity—it's about creating a workplace where employees feel a deep sense of connection to the mission, purpose, and community of the organization.

True engagement happens when employees feel inspired by their work, valued by their colleagues, and empowered to contribute meaningfully. This process begins with building relationships and trust, continues with the alignment of individual and organizational goals, and is sustained through meaningful recognition and opportunities for growth.

For nonprofit COOs, cultivating employee engagement requires a strategic approach that goes beyond one-size-fits-all solutions. Instead, it calls for customized methods tailored to the unique needs, communication styles, and motivations of each employee. By doing so, COOs can create a workplace culture that fuels passion, drives performance, and strengthens organizational impact.

Encouragement vs. Criticism

Encouragement plays a pivotal role in fueling employee motivation, while criticism, if poorly delivered, can have the opposite effect, eroding morale and diminishing an employee's sense of worth. Research in organizational psychology suggests that recognition and positive reinforcement not only boost individual performance but also strengthen team cohesion and workplace culture. This concept is often tied to the psychological principle of "positive reinforcement," where the frequency of desired behaviors increases when followed by rewards or praise.

Leaders who provide encouragement that is both specific and timely create an environment where employees feel seen and valued. Generic praise such as "Great job", while appreciated, often lacks the personal impact of more targeted feedback. Instead, effective leaders focus on recognizing the specific actions or qualities that contributed to success. For example, rather than saying, "Great job," a leader might say, "Your grant proposal was so well-researched and persuasive—it's sure to make an impact with our funders." This form of detailed recognition not only boosts the employee's sense of competence but also provides a clear example of the behaviors that are valued within the organization.

Furthermore, studies have shown that specific, personalized feedback can lead to increased employee engagement and sustained motivation. By calling out specific behaviors and their impact, employees are more likely to understand the value of their contributions and feel a deeper connection to the organization's mission. Over time, this approach fosters a workplace culture where encouragement and feedback are part of the everyday experience, driving continuous growth and high performance.

Balanced Feedback Ratios

Extensive research in organizational psychology indicates that maintaining a ratio of five positive interactions for every one negative interaction is critical to fostering psychological safety in the workplace. This 5:1 ratio, often cited in studies on effective team dynamics, creates an environment of trust and emotional security. When employees feel that their positive contributions are seen and acknowledged more frequently than their missteps, they are more willing to take creative risks, voice new ideas, and engage in open dialogue with their peers and supervisors.

The power of this ratio lies in its ability to build a sense of trust and belonging among employees. Positive interactions—such as praise, recognition, and moments of shared appreciation—become the social currency of a supportive workplace. When employees experience consistent affirmation, it reinforces their sense of value and their connection to the mission of the organization. This sense of psychological safety is particularly important in nonprofit environments where emotional labor and mission-driven work are often at the core of daily operations.

Leaders can intentionally promote these positive interactions by recognizing small wins, celebrating everyday achievements, and creating spaces for public recognition. One effective strategy is to introduce a "kudos board"—a virtual or physical space where team members can celebrate each other's contributions. This not only reinforces positive behaviors but also fosters a culture of appreciation where colleagues uplift one another. Offering genuine, personalized praise is another key approach. Instead of vague statements like "Good job," leaders should offer specific and timely feedback that highlights the exact action or behavior being recognized, such as, "Your attention to detail in the grant proposal was exceptional. The clarity of your analysis really made our case more compelling to funders."

By embedding this approach into daily operations, nonprofits create a workplace culture where trust, encouragement, and belonging thrive. The long-term impact is a more resilient, engaged, and mission-driven workforce that feels supported and motivated to achieve shared goals.

DISC Communication Styles

Every employee has a preferred communication style, and understanding these differences can significantly enhance workplace communication, collaboration, and engagement. One of the most effective tools for understanding communication preferences is the DISC personality assessment. DISC stands for Dominance, Influence, Steadiness, and Conscientiousness—four core personality types that influence how people interact, process information, and respond to feedback.

When nonprofit leaders and COOs understand the DISC profiles of their team members, they can tailor their feedback and communication approaches to meet the unique needs of each individual. For example, individuals with a **Dominance** profile tend to value efficiency, directness, and goal-oriented communication. They prefer clear, concise feedback that focuses on results and actionable steps. To engage a Dominant employee, a leader might say, "Your initiative to streamline our volunteer scheduling process saved us significant time and effort. Let's discuss how we can apply this approach to other workflows." This feedback aligns with their preference for results-driven, action-oriented communication.

In contrast, those with an **Influence** profile thrive on social connection, recognition, and enthusiasm. Feedback for these employees should emphasize relationships and positive reinforcement. Leaders might say, "Your energy and enthusiasm during last week's donor event created a welcoming environment for our supporters. It's clear you're a natural connector, and that's invaluable to our work." This approach reinforces the employee's contributions in a way that aligns with their preference for positive, people-centered interactions.

Steadiness-oriented employees prioritize stability, cooperation, and harmony. They value calm, consistent feedback delivered in a thoughtful manner. Rather than abrupt or overly critical feedback, a leader might say, "Your steady approach to managing the training schedule ensured that every new hire felt prepared and supported. Your consistency is a stabilizing force on our team." This type of feedback aligns with the Steady employee's need for reassurance and recognition of their dependable nature.

Finally, individuals with a **Conscientiousness** profile emphasize accuracy, precision, and data-driven decision-making. They thrive on logical, detail-oriented feedback that is supported by evidence. For instance, a leader might say, "Your meticulous attention to detail in the grant's financial reporting was exceptional. It ensured we met compliance standards and avoided potential audit risks." This feedback provides specific, factual information that appeals to a Conscientious employee's preference for precision and thoroughness.

Incorporating DISC assessments into onboarding, team development, and performance management creates a shared language for understanding each other's communication styles. It allows nonprofit leaders to provide feedback in a way that resonates with each employee's unique preferences, leading to more effective communication, stronger relationships, and a more engaged workforce.

Building Trust and Collaborative Leadership

Trust is cultivated when employees are granted meaningful responsibilities and empowered with decision-making authority. This sense of autonomy allows employees to take ownership of their work, fostering a feeling of competence and self-worth. When employees are given the opportunity to lead initiatives, they become more engaged in their roles and develop a deeper connection to the organization's mission.

Empowering employees doesn't mean leaving them to navigate challenges alone. Instead, it requires leaders to create an environment where guidance, support, and accountability coexist. Leaders play a critical role in encouraging open communication, where employees feel safe to voice their ideas, ask questions, and share feedback without fear of judgment. This open dialogue not only strengthens relationships between staff and leadership but also promotes a collaborative culture where innovation can thrive.

Collaborative leadership goes beyond individual empowerment. It prioritizes team cohesion, shared goals, and the belief that collective effort yields the best outcomes. Leaders can demonstrate collaborative leadership by involving employees in strategic planning sessions, inviting them to contribute to decision-making processes, and recognizing their input publicly. When employees see that their perspectives are valued and that their contributions shape the direction of the organization, it fosters a sense of belonging and trust.

Ultimately, collaborative leadership strengthens the bonds between employees and the organization. It nurtures an environment where employees feel they have a stake in the organization's success, which drives higher levels of engagement, performance, and loyalty. By giving employees the tools, authority, and support they need to succeed, nonprofit COOs can create a workforce that is resilient, mission-driven, and ready to meet new challenges with confidence.

Professional Development

Professional development extends far beyond the occasional workshop or training seminar. It is a dynamic and continuous process that empowers employees to grow, adapt, and evolve alongside the shifting needs of the organization. For nonprofit organizations, professional development serves as a strategic investment in their most valuable resource—their people.

Continuous learning allows employees to stay ahead of industry trends, master new skills, and take on expanded responsibilities. This growth directly supports the organization's capacity to remain agile and responsive to new challenges. By prioritizing development, nonprofit leaders create a "future-ready" workforce capable of addressing both present-day demands and future uncertainties.

Professional development can take many forms, from formal learning opportunities like leadership development programs and certifications to informal methods like peer mentorship and cross-departmental collaboration. Each method offers unique benefits. Formal programs provide structured learning paths, while informal opportunities foster collaborative learning and knowledge sharing.

Nonprofits that support employee development see increased employee engagement, higher retention rates, and a stronger internal talent pipeline. When employees see that their organization is committed to their growth, they are more likely to stay engaged and committed to the mission. Moreover, development initiatives demonstrate that the organization values its people, which can lead to a stronger sense of loyalty and purpose.

Ultimately, professional development is not just an employee benefit—it is a strategic imperative. By equipping employees with the skills and knowledge to meet future challenges, nonprofits can ensure they have the internal capacity to sustain their mission-driven work, no matter how the external environment changes.

Key Components of Professional Development

- **Needs Assessments**: Identify skills gaps through surveys or supervisor reviews.

- **Individual Development Plans (IDPs)**: Work with employees to create personalized development plans.

- **Learning Opportunities**: Offer workshops, online courses, mentorships, and conferences.

- **Diverse Learning Options**: Cater to varied learning preferences, from hands-on training to e-learning.

- **Resource Allocation**: Dedicate funds to professional development initiatives.

Key Takeaways for Nonprofit COOs

1. **Employee Engagement**: Foster a work environment where employees feel valued, heard, and inspired.

2. **Onboarding Builds Trust and Belonging**: A structured onboarding process supports engagement and retention.

3. **Professional Development**: Continuous learning ensures employees remain capable of tackling emerging challenges.

4. **Feedback Ratios and Encouragement**: Balance positive reinforcement with constructive feedback to sustain motivation.

5. **Tailored Communication**: Adapt communication to individual preferences to improve collaboration and connection.

By prioritizing these principles, nonprofit COOs can create an environment where employees feel deeply connected to the mission and purpose of the organization. This alignment is not achieved through a single initiative or policy but through an ongoing commitment to employee engagement, professional development, and open communication. As employees see their values reflected in the organization's actions, they become more invested in their roles, driving performance and mission impact. The result is a resilient, collaborative workforce that is empowered to tackle challenges with creativity and purpose, ultimately advancing the organization's broader mission for social change.

Chapter 10: Human Resources and People Management - From Hiring to Retention

Nonprofits thrive because of the people behind them—employees, volunteers, and stakeholders who bring their skills, passion, and dedication to the mission. These individuals are the heartbeat of nonprofit work, driving initiatives that create tangible change in communities. As a nonprofit COO or HR leader, your role in people management is not only pivotal—it's transformational. You hold the unique position of shaping a workplace that goes beyond operational efficiency to become a hub of engagement, empowerment, and mission alignment.

In this role, you're tasked with weaving the organization's core values into every aspect of people management. From hiring and onboarding to fostering a culture of belonging, your influence sets the tone for how employees experience their work. Every policy you draft, every system you implement, and every conversation you have can either strengthen or weaken the organization's connection to its mission. By prioritizing clarity, fairness, and well-being, you can create an environment where people feel seen, heard, and valued—an environment where they can bring their best selves to work each day. When people feel this connection, their commitment to the mission becomes unwavering, and the organization's impact grows exponentially.

This chapter covers the essential components of nonprofit HR management, from hiring and interviewing to retention and well-being. By following these best practices, nonprofit leaders can cultivate a workplace that attracts top talent, fosters professional growth, and drives mission success.

Section 1: Hiring, Interviewing, and Selecting Candidates

The Power of Purpose-Driven Recruitment

Unlike corporate roles that often prioritize salary, bonuses, and other tangible perks, nonprofit hiring operates on a profoundly different level. It's about connecting potential candidates to a higher calling—one that aligns their personal values with the organization's mission. While salary and benefits remain important, they are not the primary drivers for most nonprofit employees. Instead, candidates are drawn to the opportunity to make a tangible impact on their communities and contribute to meaningful change.

To attract the right candidates, nonprofit leaders must emphasize the transformative nature of the work. Job postings should clearly articulate the "why" behind the role—the specific ways the position will drive mission impact and improve lives. By framing roles as opportunities to create lasting change, nonprofits can inspire purpose-driven candidates to join the team. This approach not only attracts high-quality applicants but also ensures that new hires are intrinsically motivated to stay committed to the cause, even when challenges arise.

Steps to Build an Effective Hiring Process

1. **Define the Role Clearly:**

   o Write job descriptions that outline key responsibilities, required skills, and mission alignment.

   o Emphasize "mission impact" in the job posting to attract purpose-driven candidates.

2. **Post the Job Strategically:**

   o Use nonprofit-specific job boards, community networks, and partnerships with mission-aligned organizations.

   o Highlight the values, mission, and unique impact of your nonprofit.

3. **Screen and Interview for Fit and Competency:**

   o Use structured interview questions that assess both technical skills and alignment with the organization's values.

   o Incorporate scenario-based questions that evaluate problem-solving and adaptability.

4. **Check References and Conduct Background Checks:**

   o Verify past work performance and ensure there are no red flags that could affect the nonprofit's reputation.

5. **Make the Offer:**

   o   Provide a clear offer letter that outlines role expectations, salary, benefits, and mission impact.

Section 2: Creating a People-Centered Workplace

A people-centered workplace is more than just a trendy concept—it's the bedrock of a thriving nonprofit organization. In such an environment, collaboration, belonging, and well-being are not abstract ideals but lived experiences that shape the daily work of every employee. When people feel valued and supported, they bring their full selves to the job. They engage more deeply with their roles, form stronger connections with colleagues, and develop a heightened commitment to the nonprofit's mission.

Creating this type of workplace requires intentionality and continuous effort. It's about fostering an environment where every team member feels seen, heard, and appreciated. Leaders must cultivate a culture of inclusion, provide opportunities for growth, and ensure that well-being is prioritized alongside productivity. When employees believe their contributions matter, they're more likely to stay with the organization, advocate for its mission, and go above and beyond to achieve shared goals.

Steps to Build a People-Centered Culture

1. **Onboarding for Belonging:**

o Create an onboarding experience that connects new hires to the mission. Include "mission moments" where staff learn about the impact of their work.

o Assign mentors or "buddy" systems to support new employees' integration into the team.

2. **Build a Mission-Aligned Workplace:**

o Regularly connect daily work to the mission during team meetings and performance reviews.

o Share success stories and program outcomes to demonstrate the tangible impact of staff efforts.

3. **Provide Clarity and Accountability:**

o Set clear expectations and goals for every role.

o Use performance management tools like SMARTIE goals (Specific, Measurable, Ambitious, Realistic, Time-bound, Inclusive, and Equitable).

4. **Create Psychological Safety:**

o Foster an environment where employees feel safe to speak up, share feedback, and take calculated risks.

- o Train managers to listen actively and respond to employee concerns.

Section 3: Retention Strategies and Employee Well-Being

Retention is critical to nonprofit success. When employees leave, it's more than just a staffing issue—it's a disruption that can ripple across every part of the organization. High turnover stalls operations, drains financial and human resources, and negatively impacts the organization's culture and morale. Projects are delayed, institutional knowledge is lost, and team cohesion suffers. Onboarding new hires requires significant time and financial investment, and frequent departures can erode trust and stability within the team.

To counter these challenges, nonprofits must prioritize employee well-being. Retention strategies that support well-being go beyond salary considerations. They address the holistic needs of employees, including mental health, career development, and work-life balance. When employees feel valued, supported, and connected to the mission, they are far more likely to stay engaged and committed to the organization's goals. Investments in well-being—such as flexible work arrangements, professional development opportunities, and mental health support—can transform the employee experience and foster a culture where people choose to stay, grow, and thrive.

Key Retention Strategies

1. **Offer Career Growth and Development:**

   o Provide stretch assignments, lateral moves, and access to learning opportunities.

   o Establish mentorship programs to prepare staff for leadership roles.

2. **Non-Monetary Benefits:**

   o Offer flexible work arrangements like remote work and compressed workweeks.

   o Provide paid mental health days, wellness stipends, or childcare support where possible.

3. **Regular Check-Ins and Feedback Loops:**

   o Schedule quarterly one-on-one meetings with employees to discuss their goals, feedback, and well-being.

   o Implement "stay interviews" to understand why employees stay and address potential issues before they consider leaving.

4. **Recognition and Appreciation:**

   o Highlight individual and team contributions in meetings, newsletters, and emails.

   o Use peer-to-peer recognition platforms where colleagues can celebrate each other's efforts.

5. **Exit Interviews and Offboarding:**

- Conduct exit interviews to gain insights into why employees leave.

- Use the feedback to strengthen organizational practices and improve the employee experience.

Section 4: Employee Well-Being and Mental Health

Employee well-being is critical in nonprofit work, where mission-driven employees often pour their hearts and souls into advancing a cause they believe in. This deep emotional connection to the mission, while powerful, can also expose employees to heightened emotional demands. Over time, the weight of witnessing hardship, managing crises, or meeting relentless deadlines can take a toll on their mental health and emotional resilience.

Burnout, stress, and compassion fatigue are not just buzzwords—they are very real risks that can impact productivity, morale, and overall organizational stability. Burnout occurs when employees feel overworked and undervalued, while compassion fatigue often affects those in direct service roles who regularly confront human suffering. Left unaddressed, these issues can lead to absenteeism, turnover, and a decline in the organization's capacity to achieve its mission.

Proactive measures are essential to safeguard employee well-being. Nonprofits must move beyond reactive support and embrace a culture of ongoing care. This includes normalizing mental health conversations, offering access to mental health resources, and creating systems where employees can voice concerns without fear of stigma or retribution. By fostering a work environment that prioritizes well-being, nonprofits can ensure their people remain healthy, engaged, and ready to advance the mission with clarity and compassion.

Well-Being Initiatives for Nonprofits

1. **Promote Work-Life Balance:**

   o Establish clear boundaries for after-hours work expectations.

   o Encourage employees to take time off and model this behavior at the leadership level.

2. **Provide Access to Mental Health Resources:**

   o Offer an Employee Assistance Program (EAP) or mental health hotline.

   o Provide resources for mindfulness, meditation, and self-care.

3. **Address Emotional Labor and Compassion Fatigue:**

   o Train managers to recognize signs of burnout and offer support.

   o Implement wellness check-ins and "mental health moments" during team meetings.

4. **Foster Peer Support Networks:**

- Create informal spaces (like "watercooler chats") where staff can connect and share experiences.

- Use collaboration platforms (like Slack or GChat) to maintain connection and belonging.

Section 5: Measuring HR Success

Measuring the effectiveness of your HR strategy is essential for fostering a culture of continuous improvement and adaptability. A well-executed measurement system allows nonprofit leaders to see the bigger picture, understanding both what's working and where adjustments are necessary. HR metrics act as a compass, guiding strategic decisions and ensuring that the organization's people-related goals remain on track.

Key performance indicators (KPIs) go beyond surface-level data points. They reveal insights into employee engagement, retention, diversity, and development, which are all critical to mission alignment. By regularly tracking these metrics, nonprofit leaders can preemptively identify potential pain points, such as rising turnover rates or prolonged hiring timelines. This proactive approach not only strengthens organizational resilience but also supports a more engaged, motivated, and committed workforce.

Effective HR measurement is not a one-time effort but an ongoing process. It requires setting clear benchmarks, gathering accurate data, and maintaining open channels for feedback. When nonprofit leaders integrate these insights into their strategy, they foster an environment of learning and growth, where every employee's experience is valued and every process is open to refinement.

HR Metrics to Track

1. **Turnover Rate:**

    o   Measure the percentage of employees who leave over a specific period.

2. **Time-to-Hire:**

    o   Track how long it takes to fill open roles from job posting to offer acceptance.

3. **Employee Engagement:**

    o   Conduct employee satisfaction surveys and analyze engagement data.

4. **Training and Development Participation:**

    o   Track the number of employees who complete training and development programs.

5. **Diversity and Inclusion Metrics:**

    o   Measure the diversity of your workforce and assess progress toward EDI goals.

Key Takeaways for Nonprofit HR Management

- Hiring processes should focus on mission alignment and purpose-driven recruitment.

- Creating a people-centered workplace drives employee engagement and retention.

- Offering career growth, flexibility, and non-monetary benefits reduces turnover.

- Employee well-being must be a top priority to prevent burnout and compassion fatigue.

- Use HR metrics to measure success and refine your people strategy over time.

By following these strategies, nonprofit HR leaders can create a workplace that not only attracts mission-driven talent but also nurtures it. When employees see clear pathways for growth, feel valued for their contributions, and know their well-being is a priority, they become deeply connected to the mission. This connection transforms them from passive participants to active champions of the organization's goals. By fostering an environment where individuals feel empowered to thrive, nonprofits not only drive mission impact but also build a resilient, engaged, and loyal workforce that can sustain change over the long term.

.

Part 4: Risk, Crisis, and Adaptability

Chapter 11: Risk Management and Crisis Response - Building a Resilient Nonprofit

Risk management and crisis response are fundamental pillars of nonprofit operations, forming a protective framework that shields the organization's mission, people, and reputation. Operating within a dynamic, mission-driven environment, nonprofits face unique challenges not commonly encountered in other sectors. These challenges include heightened public scrutiny, unpredictable funding streams, and a range of operational vulnerabilities that can threaten continuity.

To address these challenges, nonprofit leaders must take a proactive approach. This involves developing comprehensive risk management strategies that identify potential threats before they escalate and creating crisis response plans that ensure swift, coordinated action when crises arise. Risk management isn't merely a defensive strategy—it's a way to build organizational resilience, inspire stakeholder confidence, and ensure mission continuity. Crisis response, on the other hand, is the nonprofit's ability to react, recover, and rebuild when faced with sudden disruptions.

This chapter offers nonprofit leaders a thorough exploration of key concepts, practical strategies, and actionable steps to master risk management and crisis response. Readers will gain insights into how to identify potential risks, establish crisis response teams, create communication protocols, and foster a culture of preparedness. By embedding these practices into their organizational fabric, nonprofits can remain agile, mission-focused, and resilient in the face of uncertainty.

Identifying Operational Risks

Effective risk management begins with a thorough understanding of the potential challenges that could disrupt an organization's operations or hinder its ability to achieve its mission. These operational risks span a wide spectrum, encompassing both internal and external factors.

Internal Risks include issues that originate within the organization's control, such as staffing shortages, technology failures, process inefficiencies, or data breaches. For example, the sudden resignation of a key team member could create a leadership vacuum, impacting daily operations and long-term projects. Similarly, a malfunction in the organization's donor database could delay essential fundraising activities and strain stakeholder relationships.

External Risks stem from forces outside the organization's control. These can include natural disasters like earthquakes, floods, and wildfires that disrupt physical operations or damage facilities. Political instability, regulatory changes, or shifts in public sentiment also fall under this category. For instance, a sudden change in government policy affecting nonprofit funding streams could jeopardize financial stability.

By identifying and categorizing these risks, nonprofit leaders can develop targeted mitigation strategies, prioritize resource allocation, and establish protocols for response and recovery. This proactive approach ensures that when a disruption occurs, the organization is prepared to respond effectively, maintaining continuity and protecting its mission-critical activities.

Categories of Risk

1. **Strategic Risks**: Risks related to changes in mission, strategy, or goals. Examples include shifts in government policy, loss of a key funder, or reputational harm.

2. **Operational Risks**: Internal risks related to daily operations. Examples include staff turnover, data breaches, or system failures.

3. **Financial Risks**: Risks associated with financial instability, cash flow issues, or loss of funding sources.

4. **Compliance Risks**: Risks tied to legal, regulatory, and contractual obligations. Examples include IRS compliance, grant restrictions, or employment law violations.

5. **Reputational Risks**: Issues that damage public trust or stakeholder relationships. Examples include negative media coverage or public backlash on social media.

Risk Assessment Process

1. **Risk Identification**: Identify possible events or issues that could negatively impact the nonprofit.

2. **Risk Analysis**: Evaluate the likelihood and potential impact of each identified risk.

3. **Risk Prioritization**: Rank risks by severity and likelihood to determine which ones require the most immediate attention.

4. **Mitigation Strategies**: Develop and implement strategies to prevent or reduce risks.

5. **Ongoing Monitoring**: Continuously monitor for new risks and evaluate the effectiveness of existing mitigation strategies.

Crisis Management Planning

A well-structured Crisis Management Plan (CMP) is a vital resource for nonprofits, enabling them to respond swiftly and effectively when unforeseen events occur. More than just a document, the CMP acts as a strategic playbook, guiding the organization through every phase of a crisis with precision and clarity.

The CMP outlines essential actions and decision points, ensuring that roles, responsibilities, and communication protocols are well-defined. From the moment a crisis is detected to the eventual return to normal operations, the plan serves as a roadmap that reduces confusion, minimizes delays, and fosters a sense of order in the face of chaos. Each role within the CMP is clearly delineated, from the Crisis Management Team (CMT) tasked with overseeing the response to the designated spokesperson responsible for public communication.

By having this structured framework in place, nonprofits are better positioned to protect their staff, stakeholders, and mission-driven activities. The CMP not only mitigates the immediate impact of a crisis but also supports long-term organizational resilience by promoting continuous learning and improvement after each incident.

Key Elements of a Crisis Management Plan

1. **Purpose and Scope**

   o **Purpose**: Clarify the purpose of the CMP and its alignment with the organization's mission.

   o **Scope**: Define the types of crises covered by the plan (e.g., natural disasters, reputational crises, or workplace violence).

2. **Crisis Management Team (CMT)**

   o **Roles and Responsibilities**: Identify the team responsible for executing the crisis plan. Key roles may include the CEO, COO, communications director, HR director, and board liaison.

   o **Decision-Making Authority**: Define who has the authority to make decisions during a crisis.

3. **Risk Identification and Assessment**

- Establish protocols for staff to report crises and conduct initial risk assessments to determine the severity of the situation.

4. **Communication Plan**

- **Internal Communication**: Outline how and when staff, board members, and volunteers will be informed.

- **External Communication**: Define protocols for communicating with the public, donors, and media.

- **Spokesperson**: Designate an official spokesperson, typically the communications director or CEO.

5. **Response and Containment**

- **Immediate Actions**: List steps to protect people, assets, and organizational integrity.

- **Containment Strategies**: Detail actions to limit the scope of the crisis and prevent escalation.

6. **Recovery and Post-Crisis Evaluation**

- **Business Continuity**: Identify procedures for resuming normal operations.

- **Post-Crisis Review**: Conduct a review to evaluate what went well, what could be improved, and what new measures should be implemented.

Emergency Response Protocols for Nonprofits

Emergencies such as natural disasters or acts of violence demand immediate, decisive action to safeguard the well-being of employees, volunteers, and beneficiaries. In such high-stakes situations, every second counts, and having a clear, well-practiced set of emergency response protocols can make the difference between chaos and control. These protocols function as a blueprint for action, guiding nonprofit staff and stakeholders through each phase of the emergency, from the initial alert to the final stages of recovery.

Effective emergency response protocols serve multiple purposes. They prioritize human safety, ensure operational continuity, and maintain trust with stakeholders. For example, during a natural disaster, clear evacuation routes and shelter-in-place procedures can prevent injury and confusion. In the case of an active shooter scenario, well-trained staff who understand lockdown procedures can protect lives. These protocols are not static documents; they must evolve over time to account for new threats, lessons learned from drills, and changes in physical environments or technology.

By establishing a culture of preparedness and ensuring that all staff are trained on emergency procedures, nonprofits create a safer, more resilient operational environment. When emergencies arise, organizations that have prepared for the unexpected can act swiftly, maintain clarity, and minimize disruption to mission-critical activities.

Types of Emergency Scenarios

1. **Natural Disasters**: Earthquakes, floods, wildfires, and severe weather events.

2. **Workplace Violence**: Active shooter incidents or other physical threats.

3. **Health Emergencies**: Outbreaks of infectious disease, such as COVID-19.

4. **Cybersecurity Breaches**: Data breaches, ransomware attacks, or hacking incidents.

Emergency Response Steps

1. **Shelter-in-Place Protocol**

   o Identify safe areas within the building where employees and visitors can shelter.

   o Train employees on when and how to shelter in place.

2. **Evacuation Procedures**

   o Designate emergency exits and establish evacuation routes.

   o Conduct evacuation drills and ensure all employees know the escape plan.

3. **Emergency Contacts and Resources**

   o Maintain an updated list of emergency contacts (law enforcement, emergency medical services, board members, etc.).

- Ensure emergency supplies (first-aid kits, flashlights, etc.) are accessible.

4. **Communications and Alerts**

- Use mass notification systems, such as SMS alerts or email, to inform employees and stakeholders.

- Ensure timely, accurate, and consistent messaging.

5. **Post-Emergency Recovery**

- Conduct well-being checks for employees and volunteers.

- Assess damage to facilities and operational capacity.

- Communicate operational changes to stakeholders.

Building a Culture of Preparedness

Building a resilient nonprofit goes beyond merely having protocols on paper—it requires embedding a culture of preparedness into every aspect of daily operations. This culture is one where risk management and crisis response are not seen as isolated activities but as integral components of the organization's DNA. Every staff member, volunteer, and leader must understand their role in recognizing potential risks and taking proactive measures to mitigate them.

Preparedness begins with education and empowerment. Staff at all levels should be trained to recognize early warning signs of potential crises and understand how to escalate concerns. Regular drills, role-specific training, and continuous improvement loops ensure that everyone is ready to act when a crisis arises. Embedding these principles into onboarding materials, employee handbooks, and daily workflows reinforces the expectation that preparedness is everyone's responsibility.

Moreover, a culture of preparedness promotes agility. When risks are acknowledged and addressed as part of regular operations, nonprofits are better equipped to adapt to sudden changes. Whether it's a natural disaster, a financial shortfall, or a cybersecurity threat, organizations with a preparedness mindset can pivot quickly, maintain continuity, and sustain trust with their stakeholders. This approach transforms preparedness from a reactive effort into a strategic advantage.

Best Practices for Building Preparedness

1. **Training and Simulations**

   o Conduct regular crisis response drills and emergency simulations.

   o Provide staff with training on de-escalation tactics and emergency protocols.

2. **Policy Integration**

   o Include risk management principles in HR policies, employee handbooks, and onboarding materials.

o   Ensure employees understand their role in crisis response.

3. **Continuous Improvement**

o   Regularly review and update the CMP to reflect new risks and lessons learned.

o   Solicit feedback from staff after drills or actual crises to improve response protocols.

Conclusion

Nonprofit leaders are at the heart of risk management and crisis response, driving efforts to anticipate, mitigate, and address the unexpected. Their role extends beyond oversight—it's about fostering a culture of preparedness, ensuring that every person within the organization knows their role in times of crisis. By taking a proactive stance, leaders can identify operational risks, develop comprehensive crisis management plans, and prepare their teams for emergencies.

The most effective leaders prioritize the protection of their mission, people, and reputation. They understand that a single misstep during a crisis can erode stakeholder trust and weaken operational capacity. To avoid this, leaders invest in training, conduct regular drills, and commit to ongoing evaluation and adaptation. Through these efforts, they build an organizational muscle for resilience, enabling nonprofits to not only survive but thrive in the face of adversity.

Preparedness is not a one-time task—it's an ongoing commitment. Leaders must remain vigilant, revisiting crisis protocols regularly and updating them to reflect emerging threats and lessons learned from real-world events. While crises are inevitable, being unprepared is a choice. By embedding readiness into the fabric of the organization, nonprofit leaders ensure that their mission can endure and evolve, even amid the most challenging circumstances.

.

Chapter 12: Facilities Management - Creating Spaces that Support the Mission

Introduction

Facilities management in nonprofits extends far beyond the basic upkeep of physical spaces. It is a strategic process that requires thoughtful space planning, resource optimization, and deliberate alignment with the organization's mission. Unlike for-profit ventures, where space is often seen as a functional asset, nonprofit spaces serve as visible representations of the mission and values of the organization. Every square foot can either facilitate or obstruct the nonprofit's capacity to serve its community effectively.

Intentional facilities management involves more than aesthetics and organization—it requires foresight, adaptability, and community-centered design. By fostering environments that are not only functional but also reflective of the nonprofit's core values, these spaces become instruments for impact. This means considering how physical layouts promote collaboration, how accessible designs enable participation from all community members, and how energy-efficient decisions align with stewardship of resources.

When nonprofits prioritize proactive facilities management, they move beyond reactive maintenance to create spaces that inspire, support, and sustain the people they serve. Such spaces become dynamic hubs of activity, fostering inclusion, productivity, and well-being. By employing evidence-based design principles, nonprofits can shape environments that empower staff, attract donors, and enhance programmatic outcomes. The result is a space that not only supports operational needs but also serves as a tangible reflection of the nonprofit's mission and vision for a better future.

This chapter explores the essential principles of facilities management, offering actionable guidance on physical space considerations, best practices for usage and leasing, and critical measures for accessibility, safety, and security.

Physical Space Considerations for Nonprofits

Nonprofits often operate within tight budgets and resource constraints, making the effective use of physical space one of their most critical considerations. Unlike larger for-profit organizations that may have the financial capacity to secure expansive office spaces or specialized facilities, nonprofits must often do more with less. For this reason, every square foot of available space must be leveraged with precision and purpose.

Functional and thoughtfully designed spaces can significantly amplify a nonprofit's impact. A well-planned environment supports efficiency, fosters collaboration, and reflects the organization's values to staff, volunteers, donors, and community members. Welcoming spaces also create a sense of belonging, which is essential for client-facing nonprofits that serve vulnerable populations. The design, layout, and usage of a nonprofit's facilities should convey a message of care, dignity, and professionalism.

When physical spaces are aligned with the organization's mission, they become more than mere locations for work—they become active participants in the mission itself. Whether it's a counseling room that provides a safe, calm environment for clients or a collaborative workspace that fosters innovation among staff, facilities play a crucial role in supporting programmatic outcomes. By treating facilities as strategic assets rather than operational expenses, nonprofits can create environments that enhance their ability to fulfill their mission and sustain their long-term growth.

1. Space Planning and Utilization

- **Needs Assessment:** Conduct a comprehensive assessment to identify space needs. Interview staff, review program requirements, and analyze future growth projections.

- **Flexibility:** Design spaces that can adapt to multiple uses. Movable walls, modular furniture, and multi-purpose areas enhance flexibility.

- **Shared Spaces:** If leasing or sharing space with other organizations, establish clear guidelines for usage, cleaning, and scheduling to avoid conflicts.

2. Design Elements that Support the Mission

- **Community-Centered Design:** Use art, decor, and signage that reflect the nonprofit's mission. For example, a youth-centered organization might showcase student art.

- **Accessibility:** Ensure compliance with the Americans with Disabilities Act (ADA). This includes ramps, elevators, accessible restrooms, and visual and auditory aids.

- **Sustainability:** Incorporate energy-efficient lighting, low-flow water fixtures, and recycling stations. These not only reduce operating costs but also align with environmental stewardship.

3. Lease vs. Purchase Decision

- **Lease Considerations:** Leasing provides flexibility and lower upfront costs. However, review lease terms carefully, especially clauses about rent increases and responsibilities for maintenance.

- **Purchase Considerations:** Purchasing offers long-term cost savings and control over the space. However, it requires significant upfront capital and ongoing maintenance responsibilities.

Best Practices for Facilities Usage, Leasing, and Shared Spaces

1. Leasing Tips

- **Negotiation:** Before signing a lease, negotiate for rent abatements, tenant improvement allowances, and favorable renewal terms.

- **Due Diligence:** Conduct a building inspection to identify potential issues with HVAC, plumbing, and structural integrity.

- **Exit Clauses:** Ensure the lease includes exit clauses or sublease options in case the organization needs to downsize or relocate.

2. Managing Shared Spaces

- **Scheduling Tools:** Use shared calendars (like Google Calendar) to reserve shared spaces and avoid double-booking.

- **Memorandum of Understanding (MOU):** Draft an MOU with space-sharing partners to clarify roles, responsibilities, and expectations.

- **Clean-Up Protocols:** Establish cleaning and reset protocols, especially for shared kitchen, conference, and event spaces.

3. Cost Containment Strategies

- **Energy Efficiency:** Conduct energy audits to identify potential savings in heating, cooling, and lighting costs.

- **Preventative Maintenance:** Schedule regular inspections and maintenance to prevent costly emergency repairs.

- **Vendor Relationships:** Build long-term relationships with reliable contractors for quick response times and potential cost savings.

Accessibility, Safety, and Security Measures

Ensuring accessibility, safety, and security is not merely a matter of regulatory compliance—it is a profound moral responsibility that reflects a nonprofit's commitment to equity, dignity, and inclusiveness. Every person who enters a nonprofit's space, whether they are staff, volunteers, clients, or community members, should feel safe, respected, and valued. When facilities are accessible, safe, and secure, they become places where individuals from all walks of life can engage, contribute, and thrive.

Accessibility goes beyond physical design elements like ramps and elevators; it encompasses digital accessibility, signage, and the removal of both visible and invisible barriers. Safety measures, from fire evacuation plans to first-aid kits, are not just best practices—they are lifesaving essentials. Security, meanwhile, protects not only physical assets but also the emotional well-being of all who use the space. By prioritizing these elements, nonprofits create environments that foster trust, support mental well-being, and demonstrate an unwavering commitment to human dignity and inclusion.

1. Accessibility Measures

- **Physical Accessibility:** Comply with ADA standards by ensuring ramps, elevators, and accessible pathways are available. Use tactile paving for those with visual impairments.

- **Digital Accessibility:** Ensure digital signage, emergency alerts, and website interfaces are accessible to those with disabilities.

- **Staff Training:** Train staff on disability inclusion and how to accommodate individuals with varying accessibility needs.

2. Safety and Emergency Preparedness

- **Emergency Evacuation Plans:** Develop and regularly update evacuation plans. Conduct fire drills and emergency response training.

- **Emergency Supplies:** Maintain first-aid kits, emergency food, water, and communication devices.

- **Compliance Inspections:** Conduct routine inspections for fire alarms, sprinklers, and HVAC systems to ensure they meet safety standards.

3. Security Measures

- **Controlled Access:** Install keycard systems, video surveillance, and secure entry points.

- **Cybersecurity:** Protect digital assets by securing Wi-Fi networks and implementing multi-factor authentication for staff logins.

- **Incident Reporting:** Create an incident reporting procedure to address security breaches, thefts, or acts of violence.

4. Insurance and Risk Management

- **General Liability Insurance:** Protect against claims of bodily injury or property damage.

- **Directors and Officers (D&O) Insurance:** This essential coverage protects board members, executive leaders, and key staff from personal financial liability that may arise from decisions made on behalf of the nonprofit. It ensures that individuals serving in governance roles are shielded from personal risk if claims are brought against the organization for alleged wrongful acts, mismanagement, or breaches of fiduciary duty. By providing this protection, nonprofits can attract and retain high-caliber board members and leaders who might otherwise be hesitant to serve. Additionally, D&O insurance supports organizational resilience by covering legal fees, settlements, and other costs associated with defending against such claims.

- **Property Insurance:** Protects against damage to buildings, equipment, and other physical assets.

Key Takeaways

- **Plan with Purpose:** Facilities should support and reflect the nonprofit's mission. Every design choice—from decor to layout—should reinforce that mission.

- **Accessibility is Essential:** Physical, digital, and programmatic accessibility ensures inclusion for all stakeholders.

- **Proactive Management:** Avoid costly emergencies by investing in preventative maintenance and energy-saving measures.

- **Shared Spaces Require Clear Agreements:** MOUs and shared calendars ensure smooth operations in multi-tenant or multi-use spaces.

- **Emergency Preparedness is a Priority:** Regular safety drills, emergency kits, and a robust emergency response plan protect staff, volunteers, and visitors.

With intentional facilities management, nonprofits have the opportunity to create spaces that do far more than house operations—they become living embodiments of the organization's mission and values. A well-managed facility communicates trust, fosters a sense of belonging, and fuels the organization's capacity to serve its community. Whether you're leasing a small office or managing a sprawling community center, every element of the physical environment tells a story about the nonprofit's priorities and purpose.

By focusing on key principles such as accessibility, safety, and strategic space usage, nonprofits can turn their facilities into catalysts for engagement and impact. Accessibility ensures that all individuals, regardless of ability, feel welcome and included. Safety protocols not only protect people and property but also provide peace of mind, enabling staff and visitors to focus on the mission at hand. Strategic space usage allows organizations to maximize every square foot of their facility, ensuring that spaces are as flexible, functional, and cost-effective as possible.

With thoughtful design, proactive maintenance, and a commitment to equity and safety, nonprofits can create physical environments that are more than just spaces— they become places where transformation happens. Every layout decision, design choice, and accessibility feature becomes a deliberate step toward supporting those the nonprofit serves and empowering staff to achieve the mission.

.

Chapter 13: The Role of Metrics - Measuring Operational Success

In nonprofit operations, metrics are the compass that guides strategy, informs decision-making, and measures impact. To succeed, nonprofits must track key operational indicators that provide insight into their financial health, program effectiveness, and organizational sustainability. This chapter explores the five essential metrics that matter most, how to create dashboards for operational tracking, and how to leverage Power BI for effective data visualization.

The 5 Metrics That Matter

Measuring the operational success of a nonprofit organization requires a thoughtful balance of both financial and non-financial metrics. These metrics act as vital signposts, providing clear insights into the organization's financial stability, mission-driven impact, and overall health. By tracking these critical indicators, nonprofit leaders can make informed decisions, course-correct as needed, and demonstrate transparency to funders, donors, and stakeholders. The following five metrics are essential cornerstones of nonprofit operational success, offering a comprehensive view of performance and growth potential:

1. **Cash Flow**

- o **Definition**: Cash flow measures the movement of cash into and out of the organization over a specific period.

- o **Why It Matters**: Positive cash flow ensures the organization can meet its financial obligations, such as payroll and program expenses. It provides a clear picture of liquidity and financial stability.

- o **How to Measure**: Track cash inflows (donations, grants, earned revenue) and outflows (salaries, rent, operational expenses) monthly. Use a cash flow forecast to predict future liquidity.

2. **Program Impact**

- o **Definition**: This metric tracks the extent to which a nonprofit's programs achieve their intended outcomes.

- o **Why It Matters**: Funders, donors, and stakeholders want to see clear evidence of mission-driven impact.

- o **How to Measure**: Use Key Performance Indicators (KPIs) specific to each program, such as the number of people served, changes in community conditions, or participant satisfaction rates.

3. **Employee Retention**

- Definition: Employee retention measures the percentage of employees who remain with the organization over a given time.

- Why It Matters: High turnover disrupts continuity and increases recruitment and training costs. Employee satisfaction is directly tied to mission impact.

- How to Measure: Calculate the annual turnover rate using the formula:

4. **Risk Indicators**

- Definition: These are early warning signs that flag potential operational, financial, or reputational risks.

- Why It Matters: Identifying and mitigating risks early prevents crises and ensures operational continuity.

- How to Measure: Use risk dashboards that track indicators such as cash reserve levels, pending grant approvals, data security incidents, and compliance breaches.

5. **Compliance Ratings**

- Definition: Compliance ratings assess the nonprofit's adherence to laws, regulations, and internal policies.

- Why It Matters: Regulatory compliance protects the organization's tax-exempt status and maintains donor trust.

- How to Measure: Track compliance with Form 990 filing deadlines, labor law adherence, and grant reporting obligations. Use a compliance checklist to assess performance quarterly.

Creating Dashboards for Operational Metrics

Dashboards are powerful tools that serve as a bridge between raw data and meaningful insights. By transforming complex information into visually accessible formats, dashboards provide nonprofit leaders with the clarity they need to make informed decisions quickly. They offer a snapshot of an organization's health, from cash flow trends to program impact, in a way that is easy to understand and act upon. A well-designed dashboard becomes more than just a reporting tool—it becomes a strategic asset that enables proactive decision-making. Here's a step-by-step guide on how to create effective dashboards for operational metrics that drive mission-focused outcomes.

1. Define Your Key Metrics

- **Align Metrics with Mission**: Ensure the dashboard reflects key performance indicators (KPIs) tied to your nonprofit's mission and strategic goals.

- **Include the 5 Essential Metrics**: Cash flow, program impact, employee retention, risk indicators, and compliance ratings.

2. Select Data Sources

- **Financial Data**: Pull data from accounting software (e.g., QuickBooks) to track cash flow and financial performance.

- **HR Data**: Use HR software or internal spreadsheets to track employee retention and turnover rates.

- **Impact Data**: Collect data from program management systems or surveys to track program impact.

- **Compliance Data**: Leverage tools that track compliance checklists and deadlines (e.g., IRS Form 990 filing).

3. Design Your Dashboard

- **Simplicity Matters**: Keep dashboards clean, simple, and focused on essential metrics.

- **Use Visuals**: Incorporate line graphs, bar charts, and pie charts to make data more digestible.

- **Prioritize Real-Time Updates**: Dashboards should pull live data to reflect current performance.

4. Customize Visuals by Role

- **Executive View**: Focus on high-level metrics like cash flow, compliance status, and program impact.

- **Departmental View**: Tailor dashboards for HR, finance, and program teams to show metrics specific to their responsibilities.

Using Power BI for Data Visualization

Power BI is a transformative data visualization tool that empowers nonprofits to convert complex datasets into dynamic, interactive dashboards. By leveraging the capabilities of Power BI, organizations can achieve real-time insights into key operational metrics, allowing for more agile decision-making and improved transparency. Unlike static reports, Power BI dashboards provide an interactive experience where users can explore trends, drill down into specific data points, and customize views according to their needs. Here's a comprehensive guide on how nonprofits can get started with Power BI and unlock its full potential for driving mission-aligned outcomes.

Step 1: Data Integration

- **Connect to Data Sources**: Link Power BI to sources like Excel, Google Sheets, QuickBooks, and other cloud platforms.

- **Automate Data Flows**: Schedule automatic updates so that dashboards always show the latest data.

Step 2: Data Transformation

- **Clean Your Data**: Remove duplicates, correct errors, and ensure data consistency before visualization.

- **Create Calculated Fields**: Use Power BI's Power Query tool to create calculated metrics like year-to-date (YTD) cash flow.

Step 3: Build Visuals

- **Choose Visual Elements**: Use Power BI's visual options like bar charts, pie charts, line graphs, and heatmaps.

- **Create Custom Views**: Develop role-specific dashboards for executives, program managers, and finance teams.

Step 4: Sharing and Collaboration

- **Publish Dashboards**: Share dashboards via the Power BI service, email, or embedded links.

- **Enable Collaboration**: Allow team members to interact with dashboards, filter data, and generate custom reports.

Key Takeaways for Nonprofit COOs

1. **Track the 5 Essential Metrics**: Cash flow, program impact, employee retention, risk indicators, and compliance ratings form the foundation of operational success.

2. **Leverage Dashboards**: Real-time dashboards turn raw data into insights, empowering leaders to make timely decisions.

3. **Harness Power BI**: Use Power BI to visualize key metrics and ensure that every stakeholder has access to the right data at the right time.

4. **Drive a Culture of Data-Driven Decision-Making**: Embed data analysis into daily operations, ensuring that every team member sees how their work supports the mission.

By mastering these tools and principles, nonprofit COOs can ensure that every operational activity is aligned with the organization's mission, fostering agility, efficiency, and purpose. When used effectively, metrics serve as a "north star," guiding decision-making and enabling organizations to stay on course even amid uncertainty. By integrating data-driven practices into daily operations, COOs can create a culture of continuous improvement and accountability. This approach not only drives better outcomes but also enhances transparency with funders, donors, and stakeholders, ultimately supporting long-term, sustainable growth and increased mission impact.

Part 5: Looking Forward

Chapter 14: The Road Ahead - Continuous Improvement for Mission-Driven Impact

The Concept of "Operational Maturity"

Operational maturity is a term often used in the context of organizational development, and in the nonprofit sector, it signifies an organization's ability to operate efficiently, adapt to change, and sustain long-term impact. Unlike "operational excellence," which focuses on peak performance at a moment in time, operational maturity is about growth, evolution, and continuous learning.

Think of operational maturity as a lifecycle. Nonprofits progress through stages of growth—much like individuals grow from infancy to adulthood. At each stage, the organization must master certain skills and processes before advancing to the next phase. While maturity can look different for every nonprofit, common milestones include:

1. **Foundational Stage**: Establishing essential governance structures, financial controls, and core policies.

2. **Growth Stage**: Scaling programs, expanding fundraising capacity, and formalizing HR systems.

3. **Sustainability Stage**: Diversifying revenue streams, embedding risk management protocols, and refining strategic planning.

4. **Innovation Stage**: Proactively embracing new technologies, experimenting with program models, and fostering a culture of learning.

Operational maturity requires leaders to continuously assess where the organization stands in this lifecycle and identify areas for growth. No matter where a nonprofit starts, achieving maturity involves building systems that are repeatable, adaptable, and mission-aligned.

Key Indicators of Operational Maturity

- **Governance**: The board provides strategic oversight, evaluates its own performance, and maintains a healthy relationship with the executive team.

- **Financial Stewardship**: Budgets are clear, cash reserves are sufficient, and risk management practices are in place.

- **Program Impact**: Impact measurement systems are established, and program outcomes are clearly articulated to funders and stakeholders.

- **People and Culture**: Recruitment, retention, and professional development strategies are aligned with mission goals.

- **Technology and Infrastructure**: Core technologies support operations, streamline workflows, and reduce the burden of manual tasks.

For nonprofit founders, achieving operational maturity requires ongoing investment in people, processes, and technology. It also means being open to change as the organization's needs evolve.

Continuous Improvement Frameworks and Models

Continuous improvement is not a one-time activity. It's a mindset and a commitment to ongoing growth. Nonprofits that embrace continuous improvement are better positioned to weather external challenges, maintain donor trust, and increase their mission-driven impact.

Several models and frameworks can guide nonprofits on this journey. Here are some of the most effective approaches:

1. **Plan-Do-Check-Act (PDCA) Cycle**

   o **Plan**: Identify areas for improvement, set goals, and develop a plan to achieve them.

   o **Do**: Implement the plan on a small scale.

   o **Check**: Measure results and assess the effectiveness of the change.

   o **Act**: Make adjustments based on lessons learned and standardize successful changes.

This cycle emphasizes iteration. Nonprofits can use it to refine fundraising campaigns, streamline HR processes, or improve program delivery.

2. **Kaizen ("Change for the Better")**

- Originating from Japanese manufacturing, Kaizen focuses on small, incremental improvements.

- Nonprofits can create "Kaizen events"— short, focused sessions where staff identify process bottlenecks and develop quick solutions.

- Example: A nonprofit might host a Kaizen event to streamline its volunteer onboarding process, reducing the time it takes to engage new volunteers.

3. **Lean Management**

- Lean principles aim to eliminate waste and maximize value.

- Nonprofits can "lean out" their operations by identifying activities that do not directly contribute to the mission. This can include reducing excessive paperwork or automating manual data entry.

- Example: By using Lean principles, a food pantry could eliminate duplicate data entry for inventory management, reducing time spent on administrative tasks.

4. **Agile Project Management**

- Agile involves working in short "sprints" where teams achieve specific, time-bound goals.

o   Nonprofits can use Agile for large projects like software implementation, campaign launches, or strategic planning.

o   Example: A nonprofit could use Agile methods to develop a donor engagement strategy by testing small, iterative marketing campaigns.

5. **Balanced Scorecard**

o   This framework helps nonprofits measure performance across four perspectives: Financial, Customer (Stakeholder), Internal Processes, and Learning & Growth.

o   Example: A nonprofit could track its performance on "Internal Processes" by measuring how long it takes to approve grant applications.

6. **SMARTIE Goals**

o   These goals are Strategic, Measurable, Ambitious, Realistic, Time-bound, Inclusive, and Equitable.

o   Nonprofits can ensure that goals are inclusive and equity-centered, a key priority for mission-driven organizations.

o   Example: A nonprofit might set a SMARTIE goal to "Increase donor retention by 20% by the end of the fiscal year, with a focus on BIPOC donors."

Each framework has its unique strengths, and many nonprofits use a combination of approaches. The key is to create a culture where staff and stakeholders are encouraged to suggest improvements, test ideas, and learn from results.

Planning for Operational Growth and Change

Nonprofits must plan for growth and change to remain relevant and effective. This requires foresight, flexibility, and a structured approach to planning. Here's how nonprofits can position themselves for growth and change:

1. **Conduct a Capacity Assessment**

    o   Use tools like the "McKinsey Organizational Capacity Assessment Tool (OCAT)" to identify gaps in areas like leadership, fundraising, and technology.

    o   Example: If the assessment reveals gaps in fundraising capacity, the organization can invest in a donor management system or hire a development officer.

2. **Build a Change Management Plan**

    o   Change management is about leading people through change. Organizations should create a plan that includes communication, training, and stakeholder engagement.

o   Example: When implementing a new CRM system, involve end-users early, provide training, and gather feedback before launch.

3. **Create a Growth Roadmap**

    o   A growth roadmap outlines key initiatives, milestones, and the resources needed for expansion.

    o   Example: A nonprofit might develop a three-year roadmap to open new program sites, with clear metrics for measuring growth.

4. **Diversify Revenue Streams**

    o   Diversifying revenue through grants, individual giving, social enterprises, and earned income builds resilience.

    o   Example: A youth development nonprofit might launch a paid online course for parents as an earned income strategy.

5. **Invest in Leadership Development**

    o   Leaders must be equipped to manage change and inspire others. Board and executive leaders should prioritize succession planning.

    o   Example: As part of the growth plan, the organization may create a "Leadership Academy" to train internal leaders to step into higher roles.

6. **Monitor and Evaluate Progress**

   o Use key performance indicators (KPIs) and OKRs (Objectives and Key Results) to track progress.

   o Example: A nonprofit may set OKRs like "Launch a new digital fundraising campaign that raises $50,000 by Q4."

7. **Communicate Change Effectively**

   o Frequent, transparent communication builds trust and reduces resistance.

   o Example: During a strategic planning retreat, share the "why" behind key changes and how each team's role supports the larger vision.

Final Thoughts

Operational maturity, continuous improvement, and planned growth are the trifecta of nonprofit sustainability. They help organizations go beyond survival and achieve lasting impact. By embedding these concepts into daily operations, nonprofits not only enhance efficiency but also strengthen trust with donors, inspire staff, and achieve mission-driven outcomes. As the organization matures, its capacity for growth, learning, and impact expands—paving the way for lasting change.

Chapter 15: The Power of Resilience in Nonprofit Leadership

Resilience is the ability to adapt, endure, and thrive in the face of challenges. For a nonprofit COO, resilience means leading with strength, empathy, and decisiveness—even when the path forward requires making difficult decisions. Resilience extends beyond personal endurance; it's about inspiring and cultivating resilience within the teams you lead. A COO must foster trust, loyalty, and a sense of shared purpose, especially when the role demands saying "no" more often than "yes" and asking people to take on tasks they may not want to do.

Drawing from my experiences as a sniper-qualified infantryman in the U.S. Army and as a COO in the nonprofit sector, I've learned that resilience starts with leading by example, prioritizing the well-being of your team, and balancing tough decision-making with compassion.

Resilience Through Leadership by Example

One of the most valuable lessons I learned in the military is that leaders should never ask their team to do something they wouldn't do themselves. This principle is just as relevant in nonprofit leadership, where actions speak louder than words. When team members see their leader actively participating in the same tasks they are asked to complete, it creates a sense of shared purpose. Leading by example fosters trust, inspires loyalty, and establishes a culture of accountability and mutual respect. This type of leadership is not performative—it's authentic. It's about showing up for the team during the most challenging moments and demonstrating that no task is beneath anyone—especially the leader. From rolling up sleeves during a fundraising event to personally engaging in crisis response efforts, these moments create bonds that last far beyond the task itself. In my experience, this approach not only builds stronger teams but also encourages others to step into leadership roles themselves, creating a ripple effect of accountability and initiative throughout the organization.

How to Lead by Example

1. Be Visible and Engaged

Whether it's a grueling campaign launch or navigating a financial crisis, show up for your team. Demonstrate that you're in the trenches with them, working just as hard to achieve the mission.

Example: In both combat and the nonprofit world, I've taken on unglamorous tasks to show my commitment to the team. It's a powerful way to earn respect and set the tone for collaboration.

2. Model Work-Life Balance

Resilience isn't just about pushing through—it's about knowing when to step back. Encourage your team to rest and recharge by doing so yourself.

Example: I make it a point to give employees as much time off as possible while trusting them to deliver on their responsibilities. This balance builds loyalty and prevents burnout.

3. Acknowledge Your Limits

Being resilient doesn't mean being invincible. Admit when you need help, and encourage your team to do the same. This vulnerability strengthens the trust that underpins resilient teams.

The COO's Role in Building Organizational Resilience

As a COO, resilience often means making tough calls—telling people "no," setting boundaries, and steering the organization through challenges. These moments test your leadership but also offer profound opportunities to build trust and loyalty within your team. Saying "no" can feel uncomfortable, but it's often necessary to protect the organization's focus and integrity. Every "no" reflects a commitment to the mission, preserving finite resources and ensuring that efforts remain aligned with strategic goals.

Steering the organization through challenges requires more than just fortitude—it demands clarity of vision and compassion for the people affected. When team members see that difficult decisions are made with thoughtfulness and transparency, they're more likely to trust leadership even in moments of hardship. For example, during periods of financial strain, clear communication about the "why" behind budget cuts can turn a painful experience into one of shared understanding and collective resilience. By consistently demonstrating this approach, COOs cultivate a culture where loyalty isn't dependent on comfort but on shared purpose and trust. The more you model this approach, the more your team will follow suit, building a ripple effect of resilience throughout the organization.

Why Saying "No" Matters

1. Preserving the Mission

Nonprofits often feel pressure to take on too much, but resilience means protecting your team and resources from mission creep. Saying "no" ensures that the organization stays focused on its core goals.

2. Empowering Your Team

Trust your team to handle responsibilities they've been trained for, even when it's difficult to relinquish control. By empowering others, you build a resilient organization that doesn't rely solely on you.

Strategies for Building Organizational Resilience

1. Clear Communication

When delivering difficult decisions, transparency is key. Explain the "why" behind your decisions to help your team understand the larger context.

Example: During budget cuts, I've been upfront about the financial realities driving those decisions while highlighting how they align with long-term goals.

2. Foster a Culture of Trust

Resilient organizations are built on trust. This means trusting your team to deliver, but also earning their trust by advocating for their best interests.

Example: As a leader, I've consistently put my team's well-being first, knowing that a supported team is a resilient team.

3. Celebrate Success and Learn from Failure

Resilience thrives in a culture that values learning. Celebrate wins to boost morale, but also treat setbacks as opportunities for growth.

Resilience in Action: Balancing Work and Well-Being

A lesson from my time in the Army that translates directly to nonprofit leadership is the importance of balancing hard work with moments of rest. In combat, I had to push my team beyond their limits while ensuring they had the downtime needed to maintain mental and physical readiness. This balance wasn't just a tactical decision—it was essential for survival. Without sufficient rest, even the most skilled team member becomes vulnerable to mistakes. In the nonprofit world, the stakes are different but no less significant. Burnout can derail a team's momentum, reduce morale, and lead to costly turnover.

In nonprofits, this means recognizing when your team needs encouragement versus when they need rest. Encouragement comes in the form of affirmations, celebrations of success, and clear communication about the value of their contributions. Rest, on the other hand, requires deliberate action from leadership. It's not enough to suggest people "take care of themselves"—leaders must actively create space for rest. This can mean adjusting deadlines, offering flexible schedules, or ensuring that vacations are truly honored as time away from work. When leaders model this behavior themselves, it normalizes rest as part of the organizational culture, rather than something that's only "earned" after overwork. By balancing work and well-being, nonprofit leaders create teams that are not only more resilient but also more creative, engaged, and ready to meet the next challenge.

Encouraging Resilience in Your Team

1. Check-In Regularly

Create space for honest conversations about workload, stress, and support. A resilient team is one that feels heard and valued.

2. Set Clear Expectations

Resilience doesn't mean working without limits. Provide clarity on roles, goals, and boundaries so your team knows where to focus their efforts.

3. Prioritize Professional Development

Equip your team with the skills they need to handle challenges confidently. Resilience grows when people feel capable and supported.

Resilience as a Personal Practice

Finally, resilience is a practice you must cultivate in yourself. As a COO, you are the steady hand during a storm, the unwavering presence that others look to for guidance. Your ability to remain composed and decisive directly impacts your team's capacity to persevere through uncertainty and change. This steadiness is not born from perfection but from preparation and practice. It's the result of building mental, emotional, and physical habits that allow you to stay grounded when everything else is in flux.

Resilience requires self-awareness and the discipline to recognize when you're reaching your limits. It's about having the courage to ask for help, the patience to wait for clarity, and the confidence to act decisively once the path becomes clear. By modeling these behaviors, you not only strengthen your own leadership but also inspire your team to approach challenges with the same fortitude. Your presence, decisions, and calm demeanor become an anchor in turbulent times, reminding everyone that storms will pass and the mission will endure.

Ways to Build Personal Resilience

1. Develop a Support Network

Surround yourself with mentors, peers, and friends who can offer guidance and encouragement during tough times.

2. Practice Self-Care

Physical fitness, mindfulness, and time away from work are essential for maintaining your energy and focus.

3. Stay Mission-Driven

Resilience comes easier when you're deeply connected to the "why" behind your work. Revisit your organization's mission whenever you feel overwhelmed.

Key Takeaways for Nonprofit COOs

- **Lead by Example:** Inspire trust and loyalty by being present, engaged, and willing to do the hard work yourself.
- **Foster Trust:** Build a culture where your team knows you have their back, even when decisions are tough.
- **Balance Work and Well-Being:** Encourage your team to rest and recharge, and model that behavior in your own leadership.
- **Communicate Transparently:** Deliver difficult news with honesty and clarity, reinforcing the bigger picture.
- **Stay Mission-Focused:** Let the organization's mission anchor you during challenging times, guiding your decisions and actions.

Resilience is the foundation of effective leadership. As an Operations Professional, you must embody and inspire it every day—not just in moments of crisis, but in the quiet, steady resolve of daily decisions. True resilience is revealed in how you show up for your team, in the clarity you bring to tough choices, and in the compassion you demonstrate when the road ahead is unclear. It's not about perfection, but about consistency and intention. When your team sees you navigating uncertainty with resolve, they're more likely to follow suit. Through your actions, your decisions, and your unwavering commitment to your team and mission, you set a standard for perseverance that echoes throughout the entire organization.

.

Conclusion: A Roadmap for Operational Excellence in Nonprofits

Nonprofits are the heartbeat of social change, addressing the world's most pressing issues with limited resources but unlimited passion. As this final chapter of *The Nonprofit Operations Playbook: Understanding Nonprofit Operations for Mission-Driven Organizations* comes to a close, it's a fitting moment to reflect on the transformative role of strong operations in driving mission impact.

This book has explored the core facets of nonprofit operations, from strategic planning and financial oversight to risk management and human resources. At the heart of every chapter lies one unifying truth: operational excellence is not a luxury for nonprofits—it's a necessity. It is the bridge that connects vision to impact, ensuring that missions are not only pursued but achieved.

Why Operations Matter

Effective operations are the scaffolding that upholds a nonprofit's mission. They ensure that the organization is resilient in the face of challenges, ethical in its decision-making, and transparent in its interactions with stakeholders. From onboarding staff to navigating crises, operations create the environment where innovation, collaboration, and impact can thrive.

Key Lessons for Nonprofit Leaders

1. Plan Strategically, Execute Tactically: Balance high-level vision with actionable steps to ensure that the organization remains focused on its goals while adapting to an ever-changing landscape.

2. Foster a Mission-Driven Culture: Align policies, procedures, and practices with core values to reinforce trust and engagement across all levels of the organization.

3. Build Resilience: Proactively prepare for risks and invest in staff development to fortify the organization against uncertainty.

4. Measure and Adapt: Continuously evaluate progress, celebrate milestones, and refine approaches to stay relevant and impactful.

Next Steps: Deepening Your Knowledge

For readers seeking to delve deeper into the practical aspects of governance, compliance, and policy implementation, my companion book, *Policies and Procedures for Nonprofit Success: A Comprehensive Guide to Ethical and Effective Governance*, offers a detailed roadmap. Together, these works provide a comprehensive toolkit for nonprofit leaders aiming to elevate their operational strategies.

If you're focused on strengthening your board's capacity for leadership and decision-making, I recommend exploring *Effective Nonprofit Board Governance: Roles, Responsibilities, and Best Practices for Committees and Directors*. This guide complements the lessons in this book by offering insight into the essential role of board governance in driving nonprofit success.

A Final Word

The journey of a nonprofit COO—or any operational leader—is both challenging and rewarding. It demands a blend of vision, empathy, and technical expertise to navigate the complexities of mission-driven work. But in these challenges lie profound opportunities to shape organizations that not only survive but thrive, transforming lives and communities.

As you move forward, remember that operational excellence is a continuous process fueled by curiosity, collaboration, and a relentless commitment to your mission. You hold the tools to make your organization stronger, more agile, and better equipped to create lasting change. Every process you refine, every policy you solidify, and every system you improve brings you closer to sustainable impact.

Thank you for joining me on this journey. May this playbook serve as a trusted guide as you continue to lead with purpose and precision.

VΘLAꝄT (Until We Meet Again),

Matthew B. Scraper
Chief Operating Officer
Owner, MBS Operations
www.mbsoperations.com

Recommended Reading

Check out other books from the Nonprofit Success Toolkit Series that can further your knowledge of nonprofit leadership, governance, and operational excellence.

By Matthew B. Scraper

1. *Effective Nonprofit Board Governance: Roles, Responsibilities, and Best Practices for Committees and Directors*

2. *From the Pulpit to the Boardroom: How I Transitioned from a 20-Year Career in Ministry to the Nonprofit Sector*

3. *Policies and Procedures for Nonprofit Success: A Comprehensive Guide to Ethical and Effective Governance*

4. *The Nonprofit Operations Playbook: Understanding Nonprofit Operations for Mission-Driven Organizations*

5. *How to Start a Nonprofit (and Actually Succeed!): A Step-by-Step Guide for Visionaries and Changemakers*